START YOUR OWN BUSINESS

After 50 — or 60 — or 70!

Lauraine Snelling

BRISTOL PUBLISHING ENTERPRISES, INC.

San Leandro, California

Printed in the United States of America.

ISBN 1-55867-007-6

Cover design: Frank Paredes

Pictured on the Front Cover
Top line, left to right: Don Stewart, Earl Thomsen, Ruth Ferguson, Lois Hitzel, Earnest Ferguson, Bob Hitzel, Patricia Pratico
Bottom line, left to right: Kay Stewart, Dr. Clifford Wold, Gloria Rickert, Louise Perkin Byer, Garry Rickert, Gladys Wold, Jean Lamb

ACKNOWLEDGEMENTS

A deep-felt thanks to all the business owners who shared their stories with me. I wish you all the on-going success you so richly deserve: Dr. Clifford and Gladys Wold, Robert Rheinhart, Babs Hicks, June Brown, Marilyn Thurau, Lee Roddy, Gloria M. Rickert, Doris Holmes, Jenny Pastor, Will and Jonnie Boudrey, Margo Burkhardt, Virginia Marshall, Ron Horner, Walter Lappert, Robert and Lois Hitzel, Donald F. Wood, W. John Frank Jr., Bob and Ruth Wearley, Richard and Doris Cook, Ray Broadbooks, Charles E. Landers, Louise Perkins Byer, Roselle Callihan, Earl Crisp, Dwight and Sharon Saunders, Florence Butcher, Vincent Messler, Carolyn B. Bolles, Robert D. Lichtman, Neil R. Cronin, Jerry Ohman, Helen Russell, Herb Rosch, Jim and Earlene Cameron, Albert Edwards, Neil Vold, Don Meecham, Bob and Jean Lamb, Etta G. Wilson, John G. Walsh, M. Jean Tooker, Earl Thomsen, Bart and Shirley Lund, Pete and Bette Horton, Charles S. Bergen, Maurice Diette, Patricia Pratico, Stanley and Vivian James, Ellen Moyer, Richard J. Dundas, Jayne and Bill Lilieholm, Rodney F. Haggett, Earnest and Ruth Ferguson, Kay Stewart, Don Stewart, Francis and Harriett Glandon, LeRoy and Lois Clauson, David K. Richards and Rick Frederick.

I'm sorry I couldn't use the stories of all those who filled out questionnaires, due to space limitations. Thanks and best wishes to John C. W. Mitchell, Sotoyome Winery; Roe and Jim Hallinan, Custom Printing & Copy; Norman Hornberger, Precision Welding; Leland and Reba Clemens, Up the Creek Realty; Dorothea Marvin Nyberg, freelance writer; C. Robert Maughan, Hildabobs; Elizabeth D. Jones, Mary Kay; Frances Wilmoth, Mary Kay; Roger E. Bennett, General Business Services; F.F. (Monte) Montgomery, Lomon Company, Inc.; Stanley C. Stahl, The Charles Cordell Company, Inc.

My special thanks goes to Ruby MacDonald who read, reread and suggested improvements, Ted Fuller who edited galleys, and Donna Albrecht who cheered me on and up. So many people were my resources in finding business people that it is impossible to mention them all. Without them the book wouldn't have happened

Dedication

This book is dedicated first to all the people who took time from their busy lives to share their stories with me.

Every one of us had teachers who made a mark on our lives. Without them to push and prod us, most of us would not be where we are today. My special thanks goes to Jen Southworth who suggested more than once that I could do anything I wanted to do if I would just focus on one thing and not try to do everything at once. Thanks and hugs, Mrs. Southworth.

Every married writer puts his or her spouse through the wringer as a book idea germinates, gets written and worst of all, when a deadline draws near. Thanks, Wayne, for putting up with fast food, a distracted companion and lights burning at all hours.

CONTENTS

1

THESE FIVE DID — WHY YOU CAN TOO!

So you're thinking about starting a business. And you're over 50. Ready for the rocking chair brigade, according to those under 30. Should be thinking of retiring and taking it easy, playing golf, according to those in their "most productive years" (between 30 and 45).

But more and more people are buying or starting new businesses after the age of 50, and after 60, and as you will see when you read this book, occasionally after 70.

Starting a business late in life isn't really new. Two ordinary people who because of their tremendous success have become celebrities, come to mind.

Col. Harland Sanders, on the skids after losing all his money, experimented with his grandmother's fried chicken recipe and fried his way into the stomachs of the American people with *Kentucky Fried Chicken*. He's known for many pithy sayings, such as, "Don't be against things so much as for things." Before he died, his promotional activities helped many franchisees make money.

Mary Kay Ash, also at a low time in her life,

developed a skin care formula (which started out as a mixture for tanning leather) into a multi-million dollar beauty industry. Her motto is "praise people to success," and her management principles have been adopted by other corporations who realize people-building is also business-building. Her book, *Mary Kay on People Management*, shows how assisting people rather than taking them to the cleaners makes for success.

But you needn't be a celebrity or become one to make your dream come true, your business grow and flourish. You need to become a magnet for information and then apply what you learn to *your* business. Experts in the field are always a good source of information.

The dozens of experts in this book are those who have done exactly what you want to do — build businesses of their own. You'll have an opportunity, as you read their stories, to learn through their experiences, which is always more cost- and time-effective than learning through your own.

Grandpa's Cakes and Cookies
Jenny Pastor

Meet Jenny Pastor, owner of *Grandpa's Cakes and Cookies*, a four-year-old firm based in San Jose, California. Jenny and her husband had owned an import business for years, but when that went sour, they were faced with a crisis.

"I've always believed you can do anything you

have to," Jenny said. "And this was a time to prove my beliefs. I looked around to see what was missing in the marketplace and wouldn't take a major investment of the money we didn't have. After tasting a chocolate chip cookie at the corner mart, I thought, 'I can do better.'"

Jenny experimented with cookie recipes right in her own kitchen. Since none of her four children ever claimed their mother was a good cook, this new venture wasn't based on previous culinary skills, but rather on need and desire. Everyone ate lots of chocolate chip cookies until Jenny had a cookie that tasted great, didn't crumble easily and yet didn't get hard as a rock either. She found the taste secret in using fresh ingredients. Then Jenny bought a few pink cake boxes, wrapped her large cookies individually, typed up labels with ingredients listed and took her product to the local gas stations and mini-markets around their house. She insisted on cash only from her customers right from the beginning, but with the provision that she would take back anything that didn't sell.

When her husband faded out of the picture, Jenny's son John became her main assistant. As their customer base grew, they mixed faster and dreamed of renting a separate facility. By the end of two years they had not only outgrown their own kitchen but were ordered to obtain the required permits or be shut down. To meet both of these needs, they moved their operation to a 480-square-foot space in a nearby office park. Their biggest acquisition was a commercial mixer. The previous owner of their new machine had been willing to take Jenny's piano plus cash in trade.

The next investment was a commercial convection oven. With these new assets, Jenny experimented with recipes for bran muffins. Again, with her credo of "I can do it better," Pastor checked out the muffins in the market. Her goal: make hers larger and more moist, which she did. Within a few months she added banana nut and blueberry, but the bran continues to be the best seller.

By the next year when *Grandpa's Cakes and Cookies* added to their customer list a catering firm which bought 3,000 cookies a week, space became critical. Jenny moved to her present location in another business park, feeling pretty "up town," since this location allows her a corner room for an office. During the same time, she increased her staff from three to eight, and gradually purchased refrigerators, another oven and a van for deliveries. She still operates her business on a cash-and-carry basis, never adding new equipment until she can pay for it up front.

The company's cookie line now includes peanut butter, oatmeal and chocolate chip cookies; the muffin side of the business includes German chocolate, lemon chiffon, cherry cheesecake, blueberry, banana nut and bran. With the new products and an ever-widening customer base, Jenny now has the opportunity to expand the business by signing on with a wholesaler or remaining the size she is.

Until now, Pastor has acquired new customers by offering samples of her yummy product personally. The cookies and muffins sell themselves, and with a money-back guarantee, few places are hesitant to try her products. Going through a wholesaler will change her marketing methods, but the challenge is in getting a company to even consider her.

"No one wants to talk to a short, fat, Spanish, over-50 woman," she said with a shrug. "I'm not exaggerating, those are the facts of life. And I don't believe in greasing palms, either. My product is unique in taste and size, and because it's individually wrapped. Now it's a case of exploring where to go next and getting John to find us a wholesale contract."

Pastor's dream is first to supply the surrounding San Francisco Bay area with her cookies and muffins and then the rest of California. "By then maybe I can give up my 100-hour weeks and begin to have a life of my own again. I could sell the company and have enough to retire on — or maybe I'll expand to Arizona — or . . ."

C. E. Associates
Albert (Al) Edwards

While he prefers to describe his service in more euphemistic terms, basically Al is a "headhunter." He finds good engineering candidates for employment in firms needing mechanical engineers with a proven track record.

Edwards and his partner, Bruce Cutright, started the business with a used computer, secondhand desks and a personally owned IBM Selectric typewriter. Only the phones were new, giving Al access to companies anywhere who might be in need of personnel. The two men have built their business over the telephone. They call company VPs, presidents, human resource staffs, all to introduce *C.E. Associates*, explain the benefits of their firm, and express their wish to be one of the final companies involved in the search for qualified employees.

Edwards credits much of their beginning success to the network of friends and business associates he had acquired during his eleven years in marketing. The manufacturing company he and Bruce formerly worked for laid both men off at about the same time. With Bruce's background in human resources, he adds a different dimension to the business.

"Having a partner has been a lifesaver, especially during the down times," Al said. "We can bounce ideas off each other and always lend the encouragement needed." In a business where they rarely meet their clients face to face, at least in this first shoestring year, that support has been crucial.

"The need for financing led us to consider Small Business Administration (SBA) loans, individuals, or a more liberal banking institution that would extend a line of credit until we were able to make some closes. This was at a time when two of our local banks were closed or sold because of take-over by the FDIC. The line of credit we obtained from a bank was sufficient since we had generated some $40,000 in revenue by the end of the year.

"The key to obtaining adequate financing was a well-organized and presented plan of action, normally known as a *business plan*. First, we prepared our expense projections, laid out a conservative income plan and clearly forecasted how long we would need the loan to sustain us. I used every resource to make the presentation a solid one, and it worked," Al said.

Since the company averages about $10,000 per employee placement, or 30 percent of that person's yearly salary, which is paid by the hiring company, there can be both lean months and others that raise the spirits. Now that the partners are getting repeat business based on their past performance of excellence, the two men feel they can breathe easier. They're planning to travel a bit to meet the people they've been contracting with by telephone.

Edwards feels that their success is based on persistence and making sure they give service above the norm. Companies have learned that they can trust *C.E. Associates* to provide stable, competent and creative engineers.

Al gives credit to his wife Laura, who has been the couple's chief financial support this last year, since he receives only a $300 monthly pension from his former company. Laura's paycheck gave Al the freedom to concentrate on a business venture that will be extremely profitable if this year's level of business is any indication.

"Did I begin the new business out of a sense of need?" Al asked. "Yes — I needed to eat and build a retirement for my wife and myself. Building a business of your own is great. I recommend it to anyone who can get into something they enjoy doing. I enjoy people and the reward here is that I can help someone improve his status by offering outstanding career opportunities."

Al does enjoy people. It comes across in his voice when he communicates through the phone as he builds Al and Laura Edwards a new lifestyle with excitement and financial security, after age 57.

Iron Door Saloon
Don Meechum

Pisek, North Dakota is smack dab in the middle of nowhere and the dying businesses around there seem set to prove the point, except for the *Iron Door Saloon* owned by Don Meechum. Now you might say that a tavern will do well anywhere, but even taverns need a steady supply of regulars. Why Pisek? As they say, "Hope the last one to leave turns out the town lights," but it won't be Don. Instead of leaving, he's building a thriving business that draws customers from a 100-mile radius to his prime rib dinners, barbecues and dancing.

Don's background in California mining wouldn't

seem to be ideal for running a saloon in the flat Red River Valley of North Dakota, but Don says people are people wherever you go. Some like to drink, some come for the food, but they all like friendly service. Which he provides.

A heart attack 12 years ago drove Don out of mining and back to his home stomping grounds of Adams, North Dakota. He knew he wanted a business of his own, but what kind eluded him. In the meantime he bought and sold farm machinery and antique cars, always watching the ads for the right kind of business.

One ad caught his attention in 1986: *For Sale, a 100-year-old tavern in Pisek.* Don looked beyond the run-down exterior and trickle-in customers to what the place could become with the right owner. While he'd never run a tavern, Meechum figured he'd spent his share of time bellying up to the bar back in his drinking days to know what it takes.

Don took his idea to the local banker and she gambled on the premise by granting him a bare-bones, five-year loan, based on the business and Don's good name, since Meechum had no money to invest himself. True, this response is unlike most ultra-conservative bankers, but her foresight was rewarded when Don repaid the loan in two years.

A gut-busting blow rocked Meechum the day he took over the building. The previous owner had thrown a huge party the night before and drank up most of the inventory. What good is a tavern

9

without a stock of booze to pay the bills?

In spite of the slow start, growth has been steady at the *Iron Door*, named after a place in the Sierra mining country of California.

"I was looking for a small operation," Don said. "I knew all my hours and energy would have to go into turning this one around and that I didn't have anyone else to depend on. The business couldn't afford extra help. Knowing that, I just did what it took, giving it everything I had."

When you walk in the door, stools lining the ten-foot bar beg you to rest a spell and let Don set 'em up for you, whatever your heart's desire.

"Wine," Don said, "didn't go over real well. Even the California varieties. This is basically beer and whiskey country."

The click of balls dropping into the pockets of the two pool tables invites you to try a game or two or you can plug the juke box, plunk your hunkus on a bar stool and swap lies with the person next to you. Or else pour your tale of woe into the ear of your friendly bartender-cum-counselor, Don.

Weekend business picked up when Meechum began serving meals. In order to do so, Don created a one-man kitchen by remodeling a closet and borrowing a few feet of space from the main room. He installed minimum equipment and hired a couple of local women to take orders. Sundays are "Standing Room Only" with the line of folks from as far away as Fargo curving out the door waiting for the prime rib dinners. When outside barbecues didn't do quite as well, Don learned another lesson. Restrict the number of items on the menu, but make sure the food is plentiful and good.

Meechum is not only the cook and bartender, but during his morning hours he turns carpenter, removing interior walls to add floor space for both the dinner and the dancing crowds. Friday and Saturday night the place is jumping with live music, so his next project is to build a bandstand area. Paintings of western and Indian scenes by two North Dakota artists now hang on the walls above the pool tables and in the dining area. Red and white checkered cloths cover the small, square dining tables. With these two additions, the *Iron Door* could almost be accused of becoming classy.

The *Iron Door Saloon* may be the only enterprise growing in Pisek, but it provides a comfortable place for customers to jaw, play pool, bend their friendly bartender's ear, or as they say on *Cheers*, ". . . go where everybody knows your name."

High Plains Travel
Florence Butcher

Florence didn't get to see much of the world as a Kansas ranch wife and mother of four children, but she dreamed a lot and made the world around her a better place because of her hours as a volunteer. That's what women did in her neck of the plains, but at age 63 Florence changed her lifestyle.

Now you can't rear children, run farm and home and volunteer full-time without developing some real organizational skills. When Florence joined the Dodge City Senior Citizens Group, they needed someone to organize a trip.

"I volunteered," she said. "I had so much fun traveling with those nice people, I set up another trip."

By the end of the second trip, she was hooked. Over the next 21 years she arranged 130 tours to all parts of the U.S. and Canada, including two trips to Nassau. Her last trip was to Texas at the age of 86.

"Most of the time we went by Trailways bus," she said. "In all those years we mainly had two drivers who drove our bus by choice. They didn't *have* to drive tours, they just liked ours. A couple of times we went by Amtrak. I had wonderfully interesting people go with us, mostly retired teachers and professional people. Everyone had such a good time that some went on lots of trips and brought their friends."

The tour groups visited unusual places on their treks besides museums and state capitols, both of which became dirty words after they'd seen so many. Tours included cranberry harvests in Wisconsin, a lumber mill in Georgia, The Leprosy Hospital in Georgia, shoe, lace and candy factories, the Purina farm in Missouri and Musk Ox in Alaska.

They visited festivals, oohed and aahed at the foliage in Maine, cogwheeled up mountains and cruised rivers. Although Florence was the leader on all the trips, she hired tour guides at various destinations to entertain and inform her travelers.

Florence collected a mailing list of about 700 people, printed brochures and arranged all the stops and starts of the trip.

"My biggest problem was getting people to reserve far enough in advance so I could book the proper number of rooms. Most folks have no idea what it takes to put a trip together for 45 people."

When computing the tour cost, Butcher would begin her calculations based on the cost of the bus and the lodging plus about $100 per person for tickets to local events. She then divided that cost by 30, the minimum number of travelers she needed to cover the expenses with some extra in case of emergencies. Then if she filled the bus to 45, which happened most of the time, she'd have some money left over. Sometimes she treated the group to a nice meal from the extra money, or she used it as a cushion for the next tour, since some did go in the hole.

"Chambers of commerce were my best resource wherever I went. They always made good recommendations as to scenic places, restaurants and lodging. After a while they referred travelers to me, too. My chamber here in Dodge City always helped me in any way they could, giving me contacts, referrals, and good advice."

Florence said making money in this business

wasn't her goal. "I know a business like this could be profitable," she finished. "But instead I had the time of my life touring this great land of ours and making sure my fellow travelers did too."

The Cameron Corner Store
Jim and Earlene Cameron

The Camerons in Bemidji, Minnesota serve a local clientele, but most of their well-known customers come in just before or after school. From the outside, this white corner store looks like a house that changed professions. But when you walk in you can't miss the main attraction. A three-by-five table, waist-high to an eight-year-old, is completely hidden by candy jars. What used to be penny candy is now a nickel at least, but the selection has greatly improved. Jars hold licorice whips, red or black; jawbreakers, all sizes; and bubble gum in every shape and flavor. Sweet tarts snuggle up to Snickers and Tootsie Pops preside over Tootsie Rolls. Even in this inflation era, owners Jim and Earlene Cameron make sure there is one jar of mixed penny candy. Every slab-sided jar sports a price card in large, plain printing: 2¢, 3¢, 5¢, up to 10¢ and 15¢, so little people can learn their numbers and with Earlene's coaching, count their purchases and identify their coins. Unaware, they even learn a little math.

"I can't stand to see them ripped off," Earlene says. "They would be in lots of other places. We're in an area that depends mostly on welfare checks. It

14

makes a good steady business for us because those checks come every month, but it's so hard to see the children start life with such disadvantages."

Little ones always sense Earlene's caring as she coaches them on their money, tries to talk them into buying more nutritious food than candy and refuses to sell cigarettes without a note from home. In mid-winter in this northern Minnesota town, she zips jackets and makes sure the children cover their ears before sending them on their way to school.

For ten years the Camerons had owned a motel. They sold it when Jim retired from the park service. According to Earlene, pushing foodstuff beats keeping after maids by a long shot. At least in this business they can lock up and go home in the evening.

They'd already done some traveling in their motor home when a friend had a heart attack. Much disturbed, Earlene insisted Jim go for a physical. It was a good thing she followed her hunch, because the doctor said Jim was about four hours away from death. The successful heart surgery put their traveling plans on hold. Never one to sit still long, Earlene began helping her son in his corner store.

As Jim recuperated, the store became his therapy, keeping him with people and busy in an easy way.

Their son sold the store to free up his parents, but he was forced to take it back after the new owners sold all the grocery stock and converted the building into a ceramics shop that failed.

Jim and Earlene bought the store from their son

and in a year-plus have built it back into a thriving business. They made some major changes, like deciding not to stock beer any longer. Their insurance premiums dropped appreciably and the money from the license went into more real food items. They've installed a microwave oven for selling hot food, expanded their frozen food section and added fresh doughnuts and cookies.

They both feel that working together in this business has been a good thing. Since there is a living area behind the store, Jim is able to rest when needed and they can cook their meals in the kitchen before heading home.

Since the wander-bug is biting again, Jim and Earlene have put the store on the market, hoping that maybe another retired person will purchase the business. The location is ideal since there are no other stores within a mile radius, and the new owners could live right on the premises if they desired.

"I'd do this again if I were younger than 67," Earlene said, ringing up a purchase. "This kind of business in a good location can do more than make just a living. I'd say this mom and pop store has been good to us." And the Camerons have been good for the neighborhood, especially the children.

TEN GOOD REASONS

For Jenny Pastor, Don Meechum, the Camerons and all the other business owners reflected in this book, a business of their own after 50 has been the fulfillment of both *dreams* and *needs*. For all, their accumulated life experiences assisted them in ways they'd never dreamed of in advance. They feel their age is an advantage, and here are the reasons:

1. All of them had been taught to work hard. The work ethic was so ingrained that tough times didn't throw them for a loop as it does many younger people. The phrase, "When the going gets tough, the tough get going," from Robert Schuller's book of the same title, applied to them many times.

2. Most people over 50 have been through some major times of recession, even the depression, so they have learned how to make do with little and stretch what they have. When times are lean in their businesses, again they don't panic. They dig in and wait the slow period out.

3. Older people understand the principle of delayed gratification. You can't always have what you want immediately. You must first have the desire, and then be willing to put in the effort to bring that desire or goal to fruition.

4. Business owners *must* understand and apply the principle of serving the customer. The famous Nordstrom Department Store that began in Seattle as one family-owned store is renowned as the leader in customer service across the United States. Their level of service used to be the norm, not the exception. The over-50 population remembers those days and knows that lack of customer service

yields a lack of customers and no customers equals no business.

5. Wisdom is usually learned and earned through many experiences in life, both good and bad. Not everyone acquires wisdom, but those who do can make successful business people. Wisdom is defined by Webster as: "The quality of being wise; the power of judging rightly and following the soundest course of action, based on knowledge, experience, understanding." The synonyms listed are: "good judgment; discretion; sagacity."

6. Usually by the after-50 years, the children are reared and gone so people can concentrate more on their business — without the distractions children can cause.

7. Many beginning older business owners have already been successful in their lives, as business owners, managers or employees. They've learned a bit about how business works and what will work for them.

8. Many people at this time in their lives have some money put aside that can be used as start-up capital; they have home equities or insurance policies and/or a stable credit history to borrow against. All these avenues of finance will be discussed later, but they are a definite benefit when dreaming of starting a new business or buying an existing one.

9. Patience is a tough taskmaster. No one is born with it, you can't buy it and you can't bequeath it

to your children. It comes with years of living and experience. Those to whom it doesn't come probably won't have the energy to start a business at any age. But the bottom line is: *patience is a must if you want to own a successful business*.

10. Persistence, the good old garden variety sort of stick-to-it-tivity, is another trait learned, earned and definitely needed. A first cousin of patience, the two go through life hand in hand. In building your business this trait is invaluable.

FINALLY

As you read, try to place yourself in the position of those you read about. Jot down any suggestions for yourself or questions you have so you can watch for answers. Make this *your guidebook* for choosing *your business*, then building, always promoting and perhaps down the road, expanding your business.

Good Reading

Her Own Business by Joanne Wilkins, McGraw Hill, 1987.
    The best features are all the forms and questionnaires the author devised. If you take all her tests and faithfully answer her questions, you'll have an excellent idea of how well-prepared you are to build and run a business of your own. Following her guidelines will take time (her questions are real soul-searchers), but could save you plenty of heartache in the long run.

2

HOBBY + CUSTOMERS = BUSINESS

Sandra Kurtzig, founder of ASK Computer Systems, Inc. in Mountain View, California, has some good advice for those thinking of the entrepreneurial life. She says, "Find a business you're excited about and work from your strengths. First you have to find out what drives you because starting just any business won't work. And you can't go into it for the money. It must be fun. You have to be passionate about making it work. You're going to be putting in incredible hours, and — if you're lucky — doing it for a long time." (From *Entrepreneur* magazine, March 1990)

As you read the following stories of people who are in the trenches, see if they aren't living up to her suggestions.

A LIFE-LONG DREAM

Some people go through life with a "someday I'll . . ." dream. Many people never achieve their dream, but others plan and work their plan until they have that dream business of their own. They learn the needed skills, set aside money, do whatever it takes to get their businesses off the ground. They are indeed passionate about their goals.

Roddy Publications
Lee Roddy

Lee Roddy is a wonderful example of someone who is passionate about his work; in fact, he refers to his business as "the fulfillment of a lifelong dream."

I heard this man speak at the first writer's conference I attended in Portland, Oregon in 1981. He talked about the writing life with passion and power as he challenged the audience to give their best in the worthy calling of wordsmithing.

"You can do it," he said when I confided my idea for a children's novel. "And let me know about the outcome." I believed him and sent him an autographed copy a year and a half later.

What makes Lee Roddy so impressive? He is a master speaker and teacher. He is obviously working hard himself, and profitably so; his sense of humor makes him a delight to be around; he always takes time to encourage new writers and he has the gift to inspire others. Would that all teachers and speakers owned those traits.

Lee began life in a poor family near Possum Trot, Illinois. He says they were so poor that while his father kept the wolf away from the door, the stork came in the back window ten times. If those weren't problems enough, Lee had a crippled leg and for years wore a shoe with a five-and-a-half–inch sole.

"Since I was crippled, I didn't have to do all the outside farm labor. Instead, I learned to read and study. It's thanks to the Shriners Hospital for Crippled Children that today I walk like everyone else."

Lee's love affair with words has gone on all his life in his various professions as newspaper editor-publisher, advertising agency promotion director, general manager for radio stations and a staff-novelist researcher for a motion picture and television production company.

All the years of writing in his spare time paid off publicly in 1977 when Lee ghosted *The Life and Times of Grizzly Adams*, which became both a movie and a prime-time television series.

The Lincoln Conspiracy, also released in 1977, hit the best-seller list and became a movie. By this time Lee had made some famous people more famous by his ghosted manuscripts with nary a whisper about who "really" wrote those books. It is only recently that titles may include a ghost's byline using "with" or "and," depending on the clout of both the ghost writer and of the well-known individual.

In 1980, at the age of 59, Lee and his wife Cicely took the giant step into full-time writing and speaking. Their accountant suggested they form a company, so they became *Roddy Publications*.

"Those first years were feast or famine," Lee said,

"with my greatest difficulty being to stabilize the cash flow. While I do well now, I still put in twelve-hour days, six days a week and if there is a deadline, more."

Lee has been most successful in writing for eight to twelve-year-olds, the type of book referred to as "middlers" or "middle reading" group. The first four books in his D.J. Dillon series, through Victor Publishers, won the 1986 "Angel" award for excellence in quality moral media.

In the series Lee takes a boy named D.J., an animal and plenty of hair-raising crises to create stories that bring a difficult audience, boy readers, back for more.

Lee's comments to would-be writers is to get your hero or heroine in deep trouble and keep the character in danger to make your stories exciting. His advice works, because the sales of his more than 50 books number in the millions.

He especially enjoys writing series, his latest being *An American Adventure Series* for Bethany House Publishers. Set during the depression era with Hildy Corrigan as the young heroine, the first two, *The Overland Express* and *The Desperate Search*, were released in February 1989 and by June were listed on the *Bookstore Journal's* best seller list.

While writing is Roddy's main form of income, he is nationally known as a seminar leader and speaker in the writing field. Anyone who has heard him once, recommends him to others and travels miles to hear him again.

Lee's favorite audiences have been in schools, where he is a frequent speaker for Young Author days, always selling a high number of books. His sales expanded even more when he added librarian and teacher conferences to his schedule. Since promotion is a major part of a writer's life, just as it is for any other kind of business, Lee uses all of his speaking engagements to sell books. Writers can usually buy their books at a discount from the publisher and then resell the books for retail or special discounts if they desire. This becomes a profitable part of their business if they are willing to put in that extra effort, as Lee has. Hauling boxes of books around isn't the easiest way to earn a living, which is why many writers just write and refuse the promotion end.

The Roddys became a true mom-and-pop business last year when Cicely left her newspaper editor job and stayed home to help Lee.

"It's been so successful," he said, "that it wasn't long before we compensated for her salary and in the year doubled our gross." They also added another computer to make her job as marketer and editor more effective.

Lee started with a standard manual typewriter, felt like a millionaire when he graduated to an electric office style machine and finally several years ago bought a computer. His computer faces a window that gives him an unobstructed view of trees, flowering shrubs, birds, squirrels, deer and turkeys without another house in sight.

While writing is a business one can get into without a steep financial investment, since beginners can learn the craft on a part-time basis, most people shy away from it because there is a fallacy circulating that you are either born a writer or you aren't. The flip side of that fallacy, just as mistaken, is that since we all studied English in school, we are all writers.

Not so.

Lee Roddy can be heard time and again stressing the need for professionalism, for taking the time to learn the skills needed for publication (for they are learnable skills), and most of all for persistent, consistent writing. He is in the process of self-publishing a series of texts designed to take the aspiring writer step by step from idea to publication and beyond. This series will be a workbook style that seems to be missing in the marketplace today.

There are plenty of places for dreamers to learn the skills needed. Lee also lectures for *Writer's Digest* and at various colleges and writers' workshops across the country. Your local library or bookstore is a good place to look up addresses and contacts, especially in a resource book titled, *The Writer's Market*.

"You can do it," Lee tells his students repeatedly. "But it takes work and commitment — plus the big P, perserverance." No one ever died from a rejection slip, they just felt that way. (Rejection slips are the notes, cards or letters saying, "No thank you" that editors send to writers.)

Lee is making his dream-come-true-business a prosperous reality and one from which he need never retire. His on-going royalties provide an income that will continue as long as his books sell, and with the brisk sale of his children's books, that can be a good long time.

You needn't be a writer to profit from Lee's advice. Persistence pays in any business, as does professionalism, and the willingness to study and learn the skills you need for your business.

START WITH A HOBBY

If building a business from something you enjoy doing is a good criterion for becoming an entrepreneur, starting with a hobby and developing it into a paying concern can be an ideal way for anyone to start a business.

Walt Disney said that a sure-fire way to success is to "do what you do so well that people will come to see you do it again and bring others with them." That's excellent advice for anyone and especially those who develop a business from a hobby. A hobby is defined by Webster as "a favorite pastime or vocation." Thus something one does for fun can become profitable. Read on and see how our experts did exactly that.

Custom Braiding
Ellen Moyer

It's folks like Ellen Moyer who keep old-time crafts and skills from disappearing. Braiding rugs, like making quilts, used to be something that most women did. Both crafts used every available scrap of fabric and created a product both useful and beautiful for the home.

While Ellen incorporates used fabric into her braided rugs, those she makes to order are always from new fabric which can be wool, a blend or polyester. Her favorite medium is wool because of its stretch and the way it molds into the desired shape.

Moyer's rugs, runners, chair mats and place mats can be special-ordered (she says she never makes larger than a 3' x 5' rug without an order), or purchased from stock she has on hand. Ellen buys remnants by the pound anywhere she can find the fabric, and uses every inch. Vermonters are known for thriftiness and she is no exception.

Moyer began making rugs in stolen spare moments on the family farm but it didn't become a business until 1985. Her production took a real upswing when her son hung a sign in her yard, as she is located on a main tourist route in Middletown Springs, Vermont. Other than the sign, word of mouth and her business card have been her only advertisements.

She says her house is full of wool and her workroom is a large wooden table. Her most ambitious project was a 10' x 12' oval, on order, of course. At first she set her prices by keeping track of the hours worked, but found that $12 a square foot plus supplies was a better system.

Ellen said, "People frequently give me fabric. Sometimes it's leftovers from a project of their own; some start rugs and give up. It takes time to learn how much to stretch the fabric in the braiding and how tight to lace it. If you're not careful, the edges curl and you get lumps in the rug. Also you have to develop an eye for color. One man ordered a large rug in tones of pink and lavender. I didn't have any of that fabric on hand, but when I finished it, everyone raved about it. I guess that's what I enjoy most, the pleasure people get from a product I love creating."

Ellen hadn't had any business experience, in fact no financial experience at all, before she began her cottage industry. She says that the best way to learn something is to find someone who knows and ask lots of questions. She has found that people are always willing to share their knowledge, but she is not adverse to paying for information when she needs to: a CPA helped her with her accounts and taxes in the beginning.

Last year Ellen brought in over $3,000 and with the orders coming in, plans on this year being even better. She is contemplating her first advertising venture in a brochure that will be distributed at all the tourist spots.

Since there are so few rug braiders around, Ellen is frequently asked to repair rugs and sometimes give lessons. She gave up selling at area flea markets and farmer's markets because her time is better used staying home braiding. That way she's available for her drop-in customers who have come from as far away as Florida and Minnesota.

Ellen's enthusiasm is contagious as she explains her business. She feels that to be successful, you should start small and grow as you gain the skills needed in your business. She sees that not only has she earned money, but she takes better care of her health, since she needs her hands and eyes to create her rugs.

"And I love meeting all the people who come by. They are always so impressed with my rugs that keeping any kind of stock past the fall, when tourists arrive in droves to see Vermont's beautiful fall foliage, is impossible. I work all winter to try to get some stock ahead, besides keep up on all my special orders."

Seat Weaving by Earl
Earl Thomsen

Earl Thomsen's business sometimes takes him into the cattail marshes, picking rushes for reweaving chair seats. What began as a hobby to redo two chairs purchased for his family home has grown to a full-time business with a continual backlog of three to six weeks. That's a lot of chairs stacked in his new workroom. They used to grace the family room.

It all started with those two chairs that needed rewoven seats. A do-it-yourselfer, Earl headed to the library for how-to books on chair reweaving. His turned out great, someone else admired them, brought in a chair for repair, and a business was in the borning.

Earl left an Illinois school district, where he had run the transportation department, for newer pastures in Vermont. He assumed another transportation position there and kept on with his chair business. By now he had expanded to cane, fibre rush, reed, splint, natural rush (cattails) and wicker repair. He learned various patterns and could identify the original design by looking at the chair.

When one becomes a master craftsman, teaching is the next step and Earl stepped.

"But most people don't have the patience for reweaving," he said. "They'd rather pay me to do it."

Thomsen's investment in this business was minimal: hand tools that include a drill press for drilling new holes when the chairs need them, a lathe to turn dowels as needed and various smaller tools. He orders most of his weaving supplies from H.A. Perkins in Connecticut, who has been in business since the late 1800s. Earl also picks rushes himself from his son's farm to restore Hitchcock chairs.

Customers are charged 60¢ per hole for seat

repair plus about $7 for the supplies. Chairs average about 70 holes, counting around the rim of the seat. Earl says he does an average size seat in about six to six-and-a-half hours. He says he'll never get rich at these prices, but he has to take into consideration the economy in Vermont.

In August, 1987, Earl had 40 chairs waiting for new seats, even though he was weaving every spare moment he had. With the decision to go full-time, he quit his transportation job and never regretted it. Fortunately his wife is a teacher, so the profit from seat-weaving isn't their sole means of support.

In order to get the business out of the family room, the Thomsens closed in the existing carport for the business and built a two-car garage for the automobiles. The $7,000 investment has been his major overhead. The business grossed over $11,000 last year with an excellent profit of $9,000. Even in laid-back Vermont, that is not sufficient to support the family, but there is plenty of room for growth and as Earl repeated, "I'm doing something I really enjoy."

Repairing wicker is a rapidly expanding portion of the business. In fact, "Wicker is coming out of the woodwork," Earl said. "People are finding their great-grandmother's wicker furniture and bringing it in to be repaired. Usually the legs are shot so I redrill the leg, insert a new dowel, rewrap it all and you'd never know the piece had been repaired. My biggest challenge is a wicker buggy a man is bringing me. He wants it restored for his daughter's wedding."

Earl says that wicker furniture frequently has a cane seat with a decorative back, incorporating special patterns: for example, *Star of David* or *Double Daisy.* He's learned to restore them all, since constantly learning new things is one of the pleasures of his business.

Another pleasure of equal importance is the privilege of hanging out the closed sign, gathering his fishing gear and taking a day off when the fish are biting, not just on a weekend.

Earl has a tight but effective advertising plan. He uses the local newspaper weekly, two county papers, the yellow pages and *The Mid-Vermont Gold Pages*, which is a directory of home-based businesses. Taking whatever he is working on and demonstrating at local farmer's markets and craft shows has drawn him business from as far away as California. Vacationers from Illinois have brought him chairs, left them over the winter and picked them up again the following summer.

Vermont encourages small businesses by requiring a minimum of licensing. Registering your business and paying your taxes are the only requirements. Earl says he's glad he left the rat race of the city for the more simple life in Vermont. He only regrets he didn't go full-time sooner.

His advice to someone interested in his business

is "to come sit with me for awhile. We'll talk while I work so you can learn all you can from someone who has the knowledge. Then, too, you can see how I deal with my customers. For no matter what you do, the customer is the key. Treat him right and he'll be back — with someone else who needs your service."

Dorian Designs
Doris Holmes

Some people look at widowhood as the end of active loving and living, but Doris Holmes is a strong advocate of the "life isn't over till it's over" theory.

"You can sit down and feel sorry for yourself for the rest of your life," she says, "or you can find something you enjoy doing and go do it."

Doris did just that. She'd been involved in artistic adventures for most of her life, but it was by accident that she created her new venture. She and an eleven-year-old granddaughter were playing at sculpting animals, but when the tiny sheep's legs weren't right, they cut them off with the idea to reattach them. Reattach the legs they did, but with pins, so the legs moved.

The little girl wore the sheep necklace they created to a birthday party, and ended up giving the dancing sheep to the birthday girl. Grandma made another one and the business idea began to hatch. Articulated legs on over 100 different kinds of animals now combine with beads and knotted cord to make wonderfully whimsical necklaces and pins.

Doris originally poured, sculpted, hand-painted and assembled the animals, and then strung the cords and beads and attached the creatures. She spoke at senior centers on the effects of positive living and thinking, showing her unique characters and selling them on a steady basis.

"I had never had any kind of business experience," Doris said, "so this was an entirely new field for me. It wasn't enough just to be an artist, now I had to decide on pricing, promotion pieces, accounting, shipping, taxes — all the stages of a business. My son Brian fell in love with my idea and took over the business side so I could continue to create. We named the business *Dorian Designs*, after both our names."

It wasn't long before Doris had to hire additional help to keep up with the demand. In order to do this she had to create a system from start to finish that she could train others to follow. There are fifteen different steps for making each animal, which run the gamut of the animal kingdom, including farm animals, wild animals, sea mammals, birds, dogs and cats with different varieties of each. She even creates one of a kind from a picture of someone's pet. These she paints and finishes herself.

Although Doris lives in San Anselmo, California, partner Brian located a studio in Los Angeles for their production line. They found that a combination of art students and retired senior citizens make the best work force. The work is intricate and takes a keen eye, steady hand, patience with a capital P and a desire for perfection. Painting eyelashes on a giraffe or the minute design on a carousel horse saddle can't be done in a hurry.

A carousel horse is four inches from nose to tail and three and three-quarter inches from the tip of his ears to the bottom of his painted hooves. Each leg moves separately, as they are attached to the body with two specially designed rivets. Your horse can be painted any color, but the one on *Dorian Designs'* vividly colored advertising packet is black with gold mane and tail and wonderfully intricate saddle and bridle. Even the backs of the animals are painted with a special design.

I wear a giraffe that Doris brought me. Seeing it is the only way I could have understood the intricasies of her creations. The decorative cord is white and the beads a combinations of browns, tans and black, setting off my long-legged charmer perfectly. Next I want a pig, then a humpback whale cow and calf and then . . . Besides, when my friends see them, they'll be envious, and they'll want. . .

In 1988, *Dorian Designs* created 200 donkeys and elephants for the presidential election. An appreciative note from First Lady Mrs. Barbara Bush is one of Doris's treasures. Besides presidents supporting their party, pediatricians distract their young patients by wearing Dorian animal pins. What tot can resist a pig or a pony with moving legs?

A third-grade teacher wrote to say she wears a different animal necklace each week so she and her students can discuss that particular animal. The children handle and name the critter and then the students write stories with animal characters.

As the business grows, Doris spends more of her time on promotional trips. Her wares are displayed in boutiques from Florida to Hawaii, but much of her business is still found by someone admiring a necklace worn by someone else and calling in an order. Some animals have even gone to Sweden. Doris says she's never worn one without someone asking where she got it. The little critters just sell themselves.

Dorian Designs has never had to do any advertising and the founders never took out a loan to finance the venture.

"The business just pays for itself as it goes along," Doris said. "We had to have business licenses, a tax number and a wholesale resale number for boutiques to be able to retail our product. We are renting additional space for our studio, and hired more staff which works on an independent contractual basis, paid by the piece. In fact, many of my staff take home more money than I do, and most of them have been with us from the beginning. Once they've completed the training course, they can take the designs home to paint on their own time if they want. We are really very flexible and that makes life pleasant for Brian, me and our workers."

Doris has seen steady growth in her business, with each quarter increasing the gross. The last quarter of '89 grossed about $20,000.

"We were really prepared for Christmas this year," Doris said, "and the sales were brisk. All this last year we've tried to stock one animal for each we've sold, so the holiday push didn't shove us over the edge. We've recently added a sales representative to our distribution system so that should expand us more. We showed at the San Francisco Gift Show this winter with amazing success and have applied to the one in New York. Sometimes there are waiting lists for years for these major shows so we shall see."

Doris's long term goal is to become so profitable that a large company will buy out *Dorian Designs* and then hire her as creative director.

"I love the designing," she said. "That is always an ongoing process. I search everywhere for high quality beads, even to Mexico, because I want each necklace to be perfect. And in this kind of business, you always need something new to show your customers."

FOR ADDITIONAL INFORMATION

There are other businesses in this book that began with a hobby and have grown into a thriving business. Read about Clauson's *Norwegian Rosemaling* in Chapter 16 and *Precious Pockets* by Jean Lamb in

Chapter 11.

If you have fun with your hobby and others appreciate what you do so much they want to buy what you make, you may want to think business. You may find your business leads to teaching others how to make one for themselves or figuring out bookkeeping and a distribution system for your own wares. While as a business you need to sell enough of your creation to make a profit, a hobby basis yields the added joy of creativity.

GOOD READING

The Magic of Thinking Big by David J. Schwartz,
Cornerstone Library, 1959. A book to help you
think bigger and more creatively. A classic for those
who dream of a business but get caught in one-
track   thinking.

3

HOSPITALITY — YOU'RE ALWAYS "ON"

The hospitality industry is a classification all its own. It takes a special kind of person to want to serve others in such a "daily" way. In this industry, service is not the key word, it is the *only* word.

HOUSING

Harborgate Bed & Breakfast
Carolyn Bolles

Guests at *Harborgate* in Brunswick, Maine have been known to ask Carolyn to wake them to see the lobster fishermen haul in and reset their traps — no matter what time. Lobstering is a seasonal occurrence to be viewed right off the end of the Bolles' dock that extends into Quahog Bay.

The Bolles hadn't planned to spend their retirement years in the hospitality field, but after their three boys left home, those two empty bedrooms downstairs begged for company. The daylight basement included a living room, bath and study which Carolyn sometimes uses as an overflow room, all with a sweeping view right off the patio and down to the water. The beds were there, the view changes daily, and all that was needed was more bedding, towels and a menu. Oh yes, and an advertising brochure which Mr. Bolles created in short order.

Carolyn opted to serve a continental breakfast with homemade muffins, so changes wouldn't be necessary in the kitchen. With only two rooms, the Board of Health didn't require any additions so the business license was all that was needed.

Besides customers, of course. Carolyn joined the local chamber of commerce and advertised in the yellow pages and several B & B promotional pieces, including one out of Washington, D.C. The Bolles have found their sign on the highway, the chamber and word of mouth to be their best advertising, so no longer continue with other promotions. Visitors to Bowdin College or a nearby military base bring them lots of business; in fact, graduation and parents' weekends are booked years in advance.

Their season runs from May through October with July and August being the busiest months. Carolyn says she looks forward to meeting new people and welcoming back others.

"This keeps me in touch with the outside world," she said. "We don't travel a lot and this way the world comes to us. We've had quite a few repeat customers so I see our age as a real advantage. We seem to relate to about any age group and I love hostessing."

Two years ago was a dull year for Harborgate and

the year before that everyone seemed to head for Europe, but gross income last year ran about $10,000. Since Carolyn does all the work herself, overhead is very low, especially since they've had no breakage or thievery. She feels this is a way for seniors to augment their income, but a small operation such as this wouldn't make a living.

Her advice to those starting a business is to check out your area and see if there are other businesses similar to yours. Find out all you can before you jump in, and make sure you have the health and energy to accomplish what you set out to do.

"I'm grateful that I'm so healthy but even more, that I'm doing something I really enjoy. I think that's the major ingredient for success."

DINING OUT

With more women working full-time outside the home, dining out has become a national pastime. Restaurants of infinite variety abound in every city and hamlet, offering enterprising folk another type of business. Again, as in the housing industry, a restaurant takes a tremendous degree of caring for people to become popular and draw the repeat traffic necessary to stay in business.

Bob's Hideaway
Bob Lichtman

"Everything fell together perfectly for this place," said Bob Lichtman, owner of *Bob's Hideaway*, a white-tablecloth restaurant in Brunswick, Maine.

"And everything we do follows the same direction. The advertising, the menus, hiring and keeping help, finding an excellent young chef whom I took in as a partner. It's as if all my years of experience jelled for this enterprise."

Bob said he was born into the restaurant business and except for a stint in the army, where he managed the officer's club on the side, and a period where he worked in textiles, all his working years have been spent in the food business. He has done it all, from waitering to cooking, from managing to consulting. There is no area of the operation that he doesn't understand and have his finger on.

"I'm there seven days a week. We opened last April and I am just now training someone to take over for me a day or two a week. I'm 72 years old and I still carry trays for the girls, but my delight in the business is greeting the guests and making sure they're content. I help them with their coats; in fact I think I'd bend down and polish their shoes if I saw a spot. I believe in service all the way. That principle needs to be the guiding light of anyone who wants to go into the food service business."

Bob moved to Maine several years ago and spent two stints as consultant/manager for two other restaurants before he started his own. In each case, he brought the businesses he managed back to profitability before he moved on.

When looking for a location of his own, he found the current site which had already been a two-time loser, supposedly the death knell of a restaurant location. The owner wanted Bob in so badly he co-signed the loan for $30,000. Of that, $27,000 was spent refurbishing the 90-seat eatery and bringing the kitchen up to Bob's standards.

When Bob started looking for a chef, he found David Lindall, a young man who had learned the chef profession by experience. The two clicked, and soon David had taken a loan against his house and invested his $90,000 in the new partnership. Now seven months later, *Bob's Hideaway* is at the break-even point, a record-setting period of growth in a business that has a high mortality rate.

But Bob knows the business. He knows that 38 percent of your volume is food costs, no matter how much business you do. He says that for his operation he needs $3,000 a week for payroll and $3,000 for general administrative expenses: that's rent, heat, lights and executive salaries. Put all those fixed expenses together and you have a break-even point of $450,000 to $500,000. After that you can count on 50 percent to be profit.

Bob and David have worked out the partnership details to benefit them both. Bob can choose to retire any time after two years, with David buying him out. David can request full ownership after seven years. They are filing to become a Subchapter S corporation (S corporations have tax advantages for some small businesses). Whatever they do, if the business continues as it has, Bob has set up a healthy retirement plan and David will continue with a prosperous business.

"I believe in a profit-sharing plan for my employees and in treating them right. High turnover in employees will break you, and most of ours have been with us since the beginning. I haven't run any help-wanted ads since last summer, just after we opened.

"In those early months I ran over budget for advertising, running about $6,000 a month. We advertised in the local newspapers, the yellow pages, tourist brochures, radio and television. In fact, CNN, the cable news station, is cheaper than the radio. When you do business, you have to become active in your community, so we joined the chamber of commerce. I'm joining Rotary and when the churches need a door prize, I give out gift certificates.

"Now that we're known, we've cut back to the normal percentage for advertising dollars, which runs about $300 a week.

"Last September we put a coupon in *The Dine Around*, a coupon book put out by the Rotary, and about 500 of those have been redeemed. We're just starting with coupons in a direct mail promotion called *Valu Pak*. Other places have had success with that. You know, 'buy one, get one free.'"

Bob's Hideaway serves an American menu with a variety of choices from beef, fresh seafood, veal and chicken to lobster in season. They serve nothing fried. Bob says they don't own a Frialator; they are not even serving French fries.

"You can do lots of creative things with potatoes besides French fries. Our entrées are sautéed, grilled or baked and cost from $8 to $15."

The special touches of a New York pickle plate, which has three kinds of pickles on it, and fresh popovers at dinner are additional ingredients for Bob's success.

The Hideaway is always open for lunch and dinner, with breakfasts only on the weekends until April, when the season begins. Then breakfast is a daily occurrence. The restaurant draws much of its trade from tourists, since it is right on Maine Highway One, but Bob caters to the locals. He said it takes about 6,000 families to support a restaurant of his type and the more high quality eating places that locate around him, the better he'll do.

"But the real key," Bob stressed over and over, "is the service. Nothing can beat a friendly smile, an interest in the diners themselves and a willingness to make each visit a special event. Your patrons will keep coming back and tell all their friends."

Big Daddy's
Jean Tooker

It's a Texas leap from banking to burgers but Jean Tooker got tired of spending her days cooped up in a bank and wanted to do something on her own. She thought of real estate, even went back to school for training, but the Texas economy went belly-up about that time. One day her business broker called and said, "Jean, I have just the business for you. It's a hamburger restaurant at Baylor University."

Never in her wildest dreams, Jean said, had she contemplated owning a fast food place. "I walked into *Big Daddy's* and it was love at first sight. The decor is '50s with jukeboxes, chrome and glass; the restaurant serves burgers and fries and is right on Baylor campus. I left thinking, I can do this."

One thing Jean knew for certain was that she knew nothing about restauranteurship, so she attended some classes through Service Corps Of Retired Executives (SCORE), an arm of the Small Business Administration, and read about business ownership. Jean said one of her favorite books was *How To Start a Business* by Cook. She studied business magazines and talked with other business owners, especially a friend who owned several clothing stores in Waco, who gave her a lot of good advice and encouragement.

Jean was able to get into her business with a minimum investment of $20,000, a quarter down and no difficulty in obtaining a loan for the remainder. The business was sound, so she was able to use it as collateral.

"I felt sure I could handle a loan this size," she said, "not like I was being buried by debt."

Jean feels college students make great workers; "When they say they'll be there, they're there." She now has a steady day-time cook, who is an older woman, but college students and one full-time young woman do the remaining cooking and table-waiting. Jean runs the cash register and lends an ear to the woes of both her help and her customers. She appreciates that when the kids go on break, so does she. *Daddy's* closes down at Christmas and spring breaks, but not during the summer.

The menu at *Big Daddy's* hasn't changed much since the '50s either: hamburgers, fries and cokes. Jean added a grilled chicken sandwich and took out the hand-dipped milkshakes because "they just weren't cost effective." She keeps a tight rein on expenses, even to posting a sign that said, "No tomatoes until the price goes down."

The secret is making a good burger and keeping a congenial place. Kids study, date, confess secrets, all the things that college students have been doing since the advent of the corner drug store.

And Jean cheers them on. "They've been great to me," she says in her Texas drawl. "I advertise in the student paper, *The Baylor Lariett*, and contribute to student activities, such as the 'pig scramble' and the 'heart run.' I donate burgers during Welcome Week and support concerts and such.

"The students buy food from 8:30 a.m. to 8 p.m. An average day sees about $400 worth of fast food slide across the counter. Last year I started paying myself wages and this year I'm going to have to look for an investment.

"I was even asked to speak at the entrepreneurial

class on campus," Jean said. "The kids were great, so attentive. We got into real discussions about business. They've made suggestions for me and I tell them how it is, running a business.

"I've learned from my mistakes," she continued. "Mainly it's been in food costs. For example, not ordering enough and having to buy from a local grocery. That drives the cost up. I dropped milkshakes, even though the kids said I served the best.

"I learned some lessons in hiring at first, too," Jean added. "There's a certain mentality with short-order cooks — they leave anytime they feel like it. I looked around for a woman my age and she's been a real saver. I'm looking into insurance for my two full-time people so they will stay with me."

Jean says those thinking of a business should do their ground work, investigate all avenues and then "just go do it. You'll never know if you can until you try. I know that I have a good, clean place and serve a good burger at a reasonable price. I'm proud of what I do and that's a key ingredient to success," she concluded. "I never dreamed I'd own a burger joint, but I love what I'm doing, and I love the students. They're the best; they *make* my business."

Lappert's Ice Cream
Walter Lappert

The first thing to remember about eating ice cream in Hawaii is that it melts fast. On Kauai, it not only melts fast — it sells fast.

Walter Lappert is the man at the helm of a thriving industry that began as a mere outlet for the "golden years" of his retirement. His first batch of ice cream was created on December 21, 1983, and ever since the gallons have been selling as fast as his Kauai factory can turn them out.

The small white factory, located on the main highway just past the town of Hanapepe, on the way to Poipu, has a retail store up front and the ice cream is made in back.

Lappert had vacationed on Kauai for three decades and retired there in 1981. But as he says, "I got bored quickly," and a little ice cream parlor sounded like a fun project.

Soon the word was out. Residents headed for that little place in Hanapepe like lemmings to a cliff. No one only came once.

Hotel executives tried the ice cream and added it to their menus. Business owners wanted to sell the delicious product in their stores. A wholesale business began which, added to the retail business, produced a volume of $30 million in 1989. That's a lot of ice cream cones.

Lappert is astounded at the snowball success of his "retirement dream," as he now ships container-loads of ice cream to Oahu and Maui.

"I see my age as a tremendous advantage," Lappert said. "I can enjoy myself, not take all this too seriously. I brought all my years of marketing to this little venture and now I see this profile of mine wherever I go. I have to keep busy, or I go crazy."

Lappert has taken advantage of the wide assortment of tropical fruits and nuts grown in the islands to add to his "super premium" (contains sixteen-and-a-half to twenty percent butterfat), the highest designation for ice cream you can have. He's used passion fruit, guava, mango, papaya, coconut, pineapple, lychee and macadamia nut to create a mouth-watering selection of island flavors. How can anyone resist a cone named *Kauai Pie*, a fabulous mixture of Kona coffee ice cream, macadamia nuts, coconut and deep rich chocolate fudge? Or *Coconut Macadamia Nut Fudge*?

Lappert has added fresh tropical fruit sorbets to the line for those who worry about cholesterol and fat. Made of 100 percent fresh fruit puree, they're light and refreshing.

"The mango sorbet is my pride and joy. This year during mango season, we peeled and pureed I don't know how many pounds of Kauai mangos. I buy fruit and purees from local farmers and import 25,000 pounds of macadamia nuts from the big island. From the mainland come 13,000 gallons of cream and other ingredients such as the chocolate and vanilla we buy from around the world."

In person, Lappert could pass for a relative of Saint Nicholas. He has the strong, slightly chunky build befitting a man who enjoys his own ice cream. When he smiles, the portion of his face not covered with white hair crinkles up in a most friendly fashion. His deep laugh is as contagious as his ice cream is addictive. Lappert's retirement uniform is a Hawaiian shirt, often set off by a stunning lei, and on his head is the same brimmed cap you see in the company logo.

While Lappert's son is taking the business to the mainland, primarily California, Walt claims his wife really runs the business. "I'm the PR man," he says as he shakes his head. "I still can't believe it. I hear of vacationers who stop at one of my ice cream parlors four or five times during a three-day visit, just to try different flavors. I'm incredibly flattered."

Lappert also added a line of fresh baked cookies of his own recipe "to keep away the boredom." *Chocolate Chip with Macadamia Nuts* is his favorite and the best seller. His newest venture is coffee roasting, with a little roastery in the back of the ice cream factory. "I make the best cup of coffee you'll ever want to try.

"How come I've grown so fast?" Lappert laughed. "I'm in a hurry because I may not have much time." For those over 50? "Get off the g– d–- golf course. If you want to build a business of your own you take out your savings and the first thing you buy is a bunk bed so you don't sleep too much. Don't ever borrow money. If you do, you have another partner always looking over your shoulder — your banker. He doesn't know what your business needs. He just wants to save his money.

"And research your field," he continued. "Is there

room for another business? Then give it everything you've got. We're too old to waste time and not have fun. You better decide to give the best product and the greatest service around. You can't afford not to. My ice cream's the freshest I can deliver — it leaves the factory the day after it's made — and my coffee? Just come try a cup. You'll be back."

FOR ADDITIONAL INFORMATION

As you can see, business size spans the spectrum. But success in the food and housing business, no matter what size, depends on both sales and service. In the last chapter you'll meet Clifford Wold, who first built a Holiday Inn through a franchise which included both restaurant and rooms. He then went on to create a food processing plant, called *Wold's Snacks*, so he wouldn't get bored. He too has plenty to say about service.

GOOD READING

How To Win Friends and Influence People by Dale Carnegie, Pocket Books, 1956. This oldie is still a goodie. Everyone *should* read this book once a year, but those in business *must*, since how well you relate to people is your greatest asset or liability.

4

YOU ARE THE HEART OF YOUR BUSINESS

The following three businesses are designated as *service* because they don't have an actual product to sell. When choosing a business, usually you'll find it easier and less expensive to get into a service business, rather than one that produces or sells a product. As you read, you'll see what I mean.

Rodney F. Haggett,
Appraisal and Consulting
Rodney F. Haggett

Land in Vermont, as in many other states, is being gobbled up by development, but Vermont has instituted some land use alternatives before the land is all gone. Farmers there can put their land into an easement program which prohibits any use but agricultural for perpetuity. Rodney Haggett, through his farm and land appraisal company, has become an expert in this specialized land use program.

"I've long been interested in protecting the viability of our agricultural investment," he said. "This program fits right into my beliefs."

He moved to Vermont three years ago, bringing

with him his appraiser's background, gained through nearly 20 years of government employment at various levels in the agricultural field, lastly that of Farmers Home Administration.

The Haggetts already owned land in the Lake Champlain area, so determined they would build a home there and go into business for themselves, using the skills of appraiser and secretary that they'd developed.

The building of house and business went neck and neck for the summer, but by fall the need to finish the home construction before winter took precedence. That winter after the house was finished, Rodney was forced to take a job with the government again to fill in. "All it did was make me doubly sure that I *never* wanted to work for anyone else again," Haggett said.

Prices for his appraisal services are based on the size of the property, with a typical fee of $1,200. Consulting fees are $40 an hour.

The appraisal package consists of about 30 pages, including documentation on soil, buildings, business stability and sales of similar properties in the area, with a conclusion of total value.

"Appraisals aren't commissioned just for selling the property," Haggett said. "Maybe the farmer wants to consolidate his debt, or borrow. It may be for estate planning purposes; there are any number of reasons to call for an appraisal."

Rodney says that his contacts with bankers, business people, farmers and friends were invaluable in beginning his enterprise. The most difficult part was letting them all know he was now in business for himself. He took out ads in the local paper, listed in special directories of small businesses in the county, and then became so busy he couldn't handle any more, an enviable position to be in.

"I see my age as an advantage," Rodney said. "In this business people respect age and experience. Farmers are cautious and want to deal with someone who's earned their trust.

"You need to find your niche in the market," Haggett advised those starting a business. "Don't try to do the same as everyone else. Be willing to do your research to identify where you and your services will do best. Use your skills in doing something you really enjoy. Then age won't make any difference."

Men's Counseling Center
David K. Richards

If you've spent your working years as a salesman for one company, when that company goes bust, you have a problem. Or else you have an opportunity. The Chinese have a saying that "Disaster is opportunity riding an ill wind." That ill wind gave David Richards the shove he needed to make a list of businesses he might enjoy or succeed with. When he narrowed the list according to investments of time, education and cost, he chose the one he'd leaned toward from the beginning; becoming a drug and alcohol counselor.

Most of the surprisingly short amount of schooling could be accomplished at the local community college. But it still meant hours of studying, intern time and introspection. It also meant a new challenge, a chance to help people change their lives. Coming from an alcoholic home himself, Dave knew the misery children carry on into adulthood if not given the tools for change.

Richards did something unusual to accomplish the training he desired. After completing the required college classes, he located a Ph.D. specialist in anger management and paid the man for a one-on-one crash course in managing anger and teaching the skills to others.

"I'll do the same again," Dave said, "but in another field. I can learn better and faster when under a mentor like this, and focus more specifically on a desired area.

"I was fortunate in that my wife supported us during my studies. She's a therapist with a solid practice helping incest survivors; adult, abused women," David said. "My goal was to counsel the husbands of those women so they could better understand and help their wives."

The dream took a nose dive when Richards required emergency surgery for an aneurysm in his brain. The surgery was not only a success, but David has minimal permanent damage which is a miracle in itself. "I spent one year recuperating," he said.

"For a long time, things just wouldn't stay with me. I'd read something and ten minutes later it would be gone. I focused all my strength and commitment on getting well again and taking one day at a time."

When he was able to return to work, he placed an ad in the phone book, contacted area mental health agencies, other counselors, and alcohol and drug rehabilitation centers. David spoke to civic, church, women's, men's and teen groups, anyone he could find to let them know of his new practice. Referrals started with a trickle, but now his client base is growing steadily.

"I work primarily with anger management, domestic violence and ACOA issues. These are Adult Children of Alcoholics, and anger is a direct result of their childhood. Most ACOA victims usually have above normal intelligence," he said. "They need it to build a solid life and compensate for their past history."

Richards recommends that anyone thinking of a business of his own do a complete prospectus which would include a marketing plan and feasibility studies. "You should talk to many people and see if there is room for what you want to do. Would other businesses support you?

"Make sure you write your findings down; seeing the numbers and words in black and white helps you define your project. The prospectus would also include a mock-up on the volume you think the business could do."

Richards found that his business hasn't grown as fast as he predicted because of the year he took off for his medical problem.

"But that's okay," he said. "I've found that some of my attitudes have changed. The material things are no longer so important. My wife and I make absolutely sure we take time for each other. And we're both doing what we like best. The positive self-talk I learned to do while I was recuperating continues to help me. I say 'Dave, you can do that,' not 'Dammit, you blew it.' We all need to learn to do this for ourselves because we are our own worst enemies. We'd never talk to someone else the way we talk to ourselves."

Dave said he's always been positive, thinking "Things will come out in the wash," and "Keep putting one foot in front of the other and you'll get there," but now he's proved positive attitudes work, in spite of or because of life's "opportunities."

Job Hunter Resume Service
Job Hunter Coaching Center
Margo Burkhardt

"Everything you put into the lives of others comes back into your own." Margo Burkhardt lives by that credo. Since she's been drafting resumes for people for 19 years, the children of her original clients are now seeking her out. She's been such an asset to the community that the Walnut Creek, California Chamber of Commerce voted her "Business Person of the Year" in 1988. Margo's planted acres of faith, good humor, caring and encouragement into the lives of others, always leading and teaching by example. Margo Burkhardt not only built herself a business, she builds people.

Margo is a prime example of the re-entry woman, a phrase unknown when she entered the work force after rearing her children and volunteering full-time in the community. Her husband called her a "do-gooder," yet employers claimed she had no work experience.

"The best sales job I ever closed was selling New York Life on hiring me as an insurance salesperson. There were only five other women in the sales force at the time. I focused on health and hospitalization because I could work with women during the day and besides, the men usually ignored that segment of insurance because it didn't pay as well as life."

Because of her association with NYL, Margo joined the chamber of commerce, was soon appointed to the board of directors, and designed a job forum for kids to help them find jobs and stay off drugs.

But Margo found her niche when she went to work for a company that prepped military officers for job interviews and drafted their resumes upon re-entry into civilian life. All her years as secretary in nearly every organization she volunteered with paid off. Margo could write descriptively and thoroughly — in a small space.

"I interviewed people face to face, after requiring some homework from them. In order to help them the most, I needed to know their purpose for their next job. Was it a stepping stone to something better? A stop-gap? Security? Did they need a large corporation for the benefits, or the challenge of lots of different experiences in a small company? Then we wrote the resume, to reflect the person and his areas of interest rather than naming a position."

Her resumes were effective, proven by her expansion from a 100-square-foot hole-in-the-wall to a large office shared with several small businesses. Margo functioned as the answering service.

"I needed steady income to pay the rent. At $10 and $15 a resume, my personal business income wasn't always consistent."

Margo carried her expertise one step beyond resumes as she coached her clients on their job search. "I never wanted to be licensed as a temporary agency or headhunter because I didn't want all the paperwork of a licensed professional. I just wanted my clients to get the best jobs possible."

Her writing skills branched out into ghost writing letters, reports and newsletters. At the same time she offered seminars: *How to Find a Job When You Don't Know What to Look For*, a good subject for re-entry women, teens and retirees. Another one, *Things You Should Know When You Want a Better Job* dealt with life in the corporate world. *How to Never Be Out Of Work* taught skills for building a business from scratch.

When Margo sold her resume business in Walnut

Creek, she had files on 3,000 clients, many of whom had used her service every time they changed jobs or upgraded their position.

"Now I'm planning to help my kids get their businesses off the ground," she said from her new home in Ukiah, California. "But some of my clients have found me and others have sent their friends. This is the kind of business you need never retire from."

To assist in her teaching, Margo wrote and self-published a book on resumes and cover letters and another for business owners is now in progress. She draws from her personal experience and says, "I put in information that I've seen work in my nineteen years, which doesn't always agree with the 'experts.'" Since her business life started after age 50, Margo feels age is always an asset, "although with my Parkinson's disease, I have to work around a body that needs some extra care. But you know, I always say that people kind of rent their bodies. And you have to take the good with the not so good.

"When you choose a business idea, ask yourself and everyone you can talk with, 'Is my idea marketable? Will my service or product be effective?' Don't stint on the research, because that extra effort could save you both money and time down the road. Another thing, too many folks charge too little for their service. I had a hard time convincing myself to raise my rates. You have to price your product high enough to cover your overhead, equipment, work space, supplies, wages and benefits if you hire help, and still give yourself a profit. If you do an excellent job, caring for your customers like you do your friends, you'll be successful. The money will always follow the business person who puts quality and people first."

FOR ADDITIONAL INFORMATION

As you can see, service businesses can be as varied as the people who dream them up. Watch your local newspaper, magazines and television for ideas. If someone is doing something unusual in another part of the country, you might make it work in your neck of the woods. Watch for needs that aren't being met or aren't being met in a successful way.

Florence Butcher in Chapter 1, Herbert Rosch in Chapter 11, Chuck Landers in Chapter 12 and Neil Cronin in Chapter 16 are further examples of service businesses. Remember that anyone dispensing information or doing something for someone else is in a service business. The list is endless.

GOOD READING

How to Start a Service Business and Make it Succeed by Kathryn Retzler, Scott, Foresman and Company, 1987. Plenty of good information for all types of businesses in a very readable style. Covers business from beginning to success.

5

FROM LOG HOMES TO HEARING AIDS — CHECK INTO DISTRIBUTORSHIPS

Many companies offer distributorships or dealerships to those interested and qualified. That usually means the distributors have an assigned territory where they may sell their product without competition from someone else in the same company. Good examples are the Ford dealer in your town, or the following two businesses.

L & M Log Homes
Bart and Shirley Lund

How would you like it if your home were always on display, used as a model for folks thinking they might like to build a Ward Log Home? What if those possible customers were supposed to make an appointment so you could pick up quick and swipe down the counters — but they didn't?

Shirley Lund doesn't turn prospects away, even though business is not always convenient. She and her husband Bart are the distributors for Ward Log

Homes in the Vermont area, although they can sell a Ward home anywhere they find a buyer. Bart is quick to add that while he is not a contractor, he can recommend several, and he will be there to supervise the construction of your log dwelling.

The materials, including logs, windows, doors and roof, come ready to assemble with instructions, much like an erector set. The six-foot, air-dried, white cedar logs are light enough that Shirley says she can lift them but doesn't make it a habit. A father and young son put up one package in 30 days by following the detailed instructions that came with their supplies and listening to Bart's suggestions.

Ward Homes come in all sizes and shapes; you could say the one-room variety went the way of the Old West. Many of the Lunds' customers are from New York and Connecticut looking for vacation homes, but locals appreciate the beauty and convenience of the pre-cut, ready-to-assembly home packages too.

Bart stopped teaching industrial arts in high schools and moonlighting in construction to retire in the wooded beauty of Vermont. His brother bought a Ward Log Home and after being amazed at the finished product, Bart and Shirley built one of their own and signed on as distributors.

The company offers training seminars both in sales and construction, so the Lunds weren't completely on their own. To sell their product, they exhibit their display at home shows and buy small classified-style ads in two magazines specifically for log homes that are distributed all over the country. One is titled *Log Home Buyer* and the other is *The Log Home Guide*. They also run an ad in the *Gold Pages*, but much of their business comes from word of mouth or the sign on the truck. Newspaper ads have not been effective, "because people don't become aware of the ad until they have already decided they want to build a log home," Bart said. "Then they ask around or check the yellow pages."

Although the Lunds haven't received much response from the *Gold Pages*, they appreciate the Home Based Business Group organized (see Chapter 16) to pass on business information and education to the members in their area.

"When people come to us they have no idea what they want," Bart said. "I ask if they'd like a cathedral ceiling, one story or two, a porch. They just look at each other and shake their heads. Selling for me is really educating the public to the packages and services Ward Homes offers."

"One of the things we've learned," Shirley added, "is that you don't get a second chance to make a first impression, so we try really hard to reach out to others everywhere we go. We like people; we like helping them realize their dreams of a special home. And we like working together where we can be busy at times but take off at others. This is a good business for retirees like us. You don't have a major investment and we lived on our pension while we got the business off the ground."

Southwest Hearing Aid Center
Ray Broadbooks

Ray found life boring after he retired from his years as a civilian working for the Kansas National Guard. Now was his chance to do something for himself, but what?

Since his own hearing had deteriorated, he knew how others felt who say "What?" or "Excuse me, would you repeat that?" in nearly every conversation.

"Society treats you as if you're stupid or dim if you can't hear," he said. "You find it easier to withdraw or just nod rather than making the tiring effort to communicate. I knew how much I appreciated the hearing aids I'd found so I wanted to help others in the same boat."

Ray had absolutely no background in the field, but investigation taught him plenty. He found he could get all the training he needed from the companies who design and market the product. Not only did he need to learn all about the hearing aids themselves, but how to use the diagnostic and testing equipment. Since there are many complicated reasons for hearing loss, he needed to understand how the ear functions and how sound is transmitted to the brain.

The excitement grew for Ray as he realized the

uniqueness of each case. He worked with several different companies because he wanted to provide the best aid possible for his clients and friends in Dodge City. He not only became an expert hearing aid fitter, but learned to repair and service the aids he sold.

Besides the initial training, Ray had to continually update his knowledge as the industry improved. He passed the Kansas Licensing Board, one of the most thorough in the country, and traveled around the country attending all the classes and conventions he could to keep his information current.

The technology for assisting the hearing impaired improved dramatically in the 15 years Ray was in business. The aids became smaller so they weren't so obvious, adding to the self-esteem of the wearer. As performance improved, more border-line hearing impaired found their lives enhanced.

Ray took out a small loan of $3,000 in the beginning, but soon paid that off, and the business grew.

"That's why I kept my job at the phone company," Mrs. Broadbook laughed. "We needed the income until Ray became established since he wasn't eligible for his pension yet."

Ray credits his success to *service*. He took care of his clients, went to them in an emergency, listened well to tales of woe, and always lived up to his commitments. People in Dodge City and the surrounding country knew they could trust him.

"Word of mouth was our best advertising. People

told their friends what a good job I'd done for them," Ray said.

When the Broadbooks decided to retire again, they sold the business, and holding the contract has continued to add to their retirement benefits.

"The best part of the business," Ray says, "was all the people we met. In 1981 my wife retired and helped me in the office. Those first years I really beat the bushes for clients, but after that they came to me. Many of our clients are still our friends, as are people in the companies we dealt with."

FOR ADDITIONAL INFORMATION

As you can see, distributorships can vary according to the company. In some cases the business owner orders the product which is shipped directly to the customer. In other cases inventory is purchased and displayed by the distributor, and then sold and delivered to the customer. If you know of a product you'd like to distribute, contact the parent company to learn their system. You can always find company addresses at the library if there is no outlet near you.

Marilyn Thurau in Chapter 13 is another good example of a thriving distributorship.

GOOD READING

Growing a Business by Paul Hawken, Fireside Books (Simon and Schuster),1987. Contains extensive information gleaned from Hawken's years in business, starting and building two separate companies.

6

MANUFACTURING MAY BE FOR YOU

Webster defines manufacturing as "the making of goods and articles by hand or, especially, by machinery, often on a large scale and with division of labor." Today our industrialized nation runs the gamut from cottage to billion-dollar industries with all sizes in between. Good old American ingenuity is alive and well, in spite of all the doom and gloom economists wail.

If you decide to make something to sell, you will be part of this business category called manufacturing. Read on for a classic example.

80/20, Inc.
Donald F. Wood

Don Wood chose his company name from the Perato principle: "We accomplish about 80 percent of our work in about 20 percent of our time." This company that he owns with two of his sons designs and produces automation systems for other industries.

This is not the first company Wood has started. Three years ago he set his third son, an engineer, up in a small machine tool company to the tune of $250,000. Within a short period of time, his second son, with a management/marketing background, joined the group and his sons' business took off.

Don says he dreamed of owning *his* own business all his life — "it was predestined." But he was having fun making more than sufficient money in his own profession, also associated with marketing tool products. The need, financial and emotional, wasn't great enough for him to take the leap of faith and go out on his own. His background includes all phases of the tool industry, designing, manufacturing, management, and marketing. In the last six years he had brought the company he worked for from $6 million in sales to $20 million, but the more successful that family-owned business became, the less room there was for anyone outside the family.

"You can't live off a W-2 form," Don said. "Taxes were eating all my gains so I knew I had to do something else. I took all my years of experience and started doing for other businesses as a consultant, what I had done for my former employers."

At the same time, his sons' tool manufacturing business wasn't doing as well as they'd hoped, so they sold their product line but kept the tools, with the idea that they would now go into business with their father. Don brought his seminar skills into the package and the three organized the new corporation, *80/20, Inc.*

"I visit businesses," Don said, "and convince management that they have a problem for which I can build a solution. We design and build an automation system for any type of factory that has a production line. Think of your hand, you have a gripper, your wrist, you have a rotary actuator, your arm, you have a thruster. You push, pull, lift, turn, flex. We create machines to do those skills faster, more accurately, with greater strength and consistency at far less cost than hiring manpower."

When they began looking for a location, the Enterprise Zone, a new business park in Fort Wayne, Indiana was a natural. It had central services such as secretarial and accounting, and office machines, that were paid for on a per use basis. It had high visiblity with special incentives in the way of taxes, inducements for employee training, and a great deal of support from the city fathers in their city of a quarter of a million people. In addition, they could lease the 4,000 square feet they needed at a reasonable cost.

"Besides," Don added, "there's a great synergysm with the other business owners in the center, a kind of a start-up attitude and an energy that boosts us all. But at the rate we're growing we probably won't be in this location over a year."

Don is fortunate that he has been able to fund his growing company himself and not be at the mercy of bankers who try to control their borrowers.

"So many of the current bankers are young.

Maybe they have an accounting degree but have never hired personnel or sold anything, never met a payroll. They're more like purchasing agents with no courage. The hard part of starting a business when you're my age," Don continued, "is that you've seen it all. I've become a bit of a cynic, especially about people who think they're bigger or better than the rest of us. There's nothing worse than reading your own press and believing it."

Don believes that the advantages of starting a business after 50 are tremendous. "You can have a sixth sense about what to do, using the accumulation of all you've learned through the years. You have confidence both in yourself and what you're trying to do, you know what will work and what won't. And by this time, you should have learned to listen to and trust your gut feelings.

"I see my age as a great advantage as compared to my sons who are in their 30s. They're opinionated, stubborn and rather anxious. Much like I was at their age, but we're a great team."

While Don's consulting business is over two years old, *80/20, Inc.* is only six months young. In that time, the Woods have taken production from zero to $10,000 a month with 50 percent of their factory automation systems sold and producing within a 300-mile radius, just like Don promised they would.

"We set up our business plan to be at $10 million in five years with half a million this first twelve months. That's a realistic goal and right now we're ahead of projections. By the end of the year we should have fifteen employees. We don't have trouble finding good help either, because we're in an exciting business. Talent always gravitates to forward motion and excitement."

Don's sons, Doug and John, do all the management on a day-to-day basis while their father's off around the country. "That's one of the things that keeps me happy and enthusiastic," Don said. "Besides which I have a ball with my boys. We genuinely like working together."

80/20, Inc. is unusual in that the company hasn't spent money for advertising. They depend on press releases to industry magazines: a large publication company called Pent produces 30 industrial publications. Don's well-written press releases, including *80/20's* own photography, have appeared regularly in several of those publications.

"Our business is a solution looking for a problem," Don said. "Once factory owners see our solution, they can't solve their problem fast enough. We are sold through demonstration, contact and word of mouth. Our customers keep coming back."

Don and *80/20, Inc.* are looking at the world market after they reach about $5 million in sales, with an eye toward the opening Eastern Europe block. He'd like to be a part of bringing those countries into the new century.

His advice to all business owners is "do what you know. Otherwise you'll crash and burn. Also make sure your personal human machinery is in shape. Health is everything. It takes a tremendous amount of energy to build a business."

FOR ADDITIONAL INFORMATION

I'm sure if you asked various people in this book about their "manufacturing" system, they'd look at you like you'd left your marbles home under the bed. But according to Webster's definition, Ellen Moyer and Doris Holmes in Chapter 2, Walter Lappert in Chapter 3, Jean Lamb in Chapter 11 and the Clausons in Chapter 16 are all manufacturers. You need to decide if you want to make something, sell something someone else made or provide a service. How's your list-making coming?

GOOD READING

Entrepreneur Magazine, P.O. Box 19787, Irvine, CA 92713-9440. You can purchase the latest copy at your bookstore. Their articles are excellent. Their advertising leans heavily on franchises but don't let that overwhelm you.

7

SALES WITHOUT A STORE — BUYING MADE EASY

The method of delivering their products to the consumer is a unique element of the businesses in this chapter.

An explanation of the usual system would go like this: you start with raw goods at the beginning, say wheat for example. The wheat is harvested by the farmer and shipped to a broker; the broker sells the wheat to a mill where the wheat is ground into flour; the flour is sold to a bakery and made into bread; the bread is sold to a grocery store where the consumer buys it. This system is shortened or lengthened according to the middle steps needed between raw goods and consumer. Everyone in the chain makes money on their contribution, which adds to the cost of the product to the consumer.

Let's look now at various examples of marketing methods.

MULTI-LEVEL MARKETING

No list of possible businesses would be complete without the addition of multi-level marketing

(MLM), in which field Amway Corporation is the acknowledged granddaddy. The advantages of beginning a business based on MLM are a low initial financial investment, the possibility of starting part-time while you continue with your present job, and earning while you learn. In this instance you usually work out of the convenience of your home and benefit from the tax advantages of that arrangement. MLMs are frequently dubbed "get-rich-quick schemes," but those who work with sound companies, carefully following the principles, can become wealthy through this marketing plan.

Multi-level marketing is a process of moving a product from production to consumer through a line of sponsored distributors rather than by the conventional system of raw goods to producer to packager to warehouse to store to consumer. The simplified system allows participants to make a profit without investing huge amounts of cash and at the same time assist each other through personal training and the distribution of the product.

Various kinds of MLMs have made their splash and disappeared — Cambridge, no-run hosiery, food and automobile products. The list is long.

Others such as Shaklee, Herbalife and Amway have stood the test of time. Right now FundAmerica is growing rapidly, as are others that have yet to prove themselves.

Leading colleges, Harvard Business School a good example, are offering classes in this relatively new form of business where anyone who works the system can win. The Naisbitt book, *Megatrends*, suggests that multi-level marketing is the '90s' way of doing business.

As with any other new system, there have been problems with get-rich-quickers who ended up building illegal pyramid scams where those "who got in on the ground floor" made money and those later got taken to the cleaners. The government now has stringent regulations governing this form of commerce, so anyone can check with the Better Business Bureau about new companies.

Hitzel Enterprises
Bob and Lois Hitzel

Like many other people in their age group, the Hitzels thought they were fairly well off. They owned a nice house with a pool in Norridge, Illinois, drove late model cars, had put their children through college, married them off and now dreamed of Bob's retiring from the printing company at age 60. The glow lasted until they realized his pension would be about half what they were making at that point. A change of lifestyle hadn't been part of their dream.

Their daughter Cathy and her husband Cliff had already retired because they had earned the high and profitable level of Diamond Distributor (success levels are designated by gem stones) in their Amway business. When Cliff showed the Hitzels the

Amway Sales and Marketing Plan a second time, the parents listened. That was eight years ago and Bob says they didn't break any speed records.

"Maybe if our need had been greater, we'd have pushed ourselves harder," he said. "I showed the plan to most of our friends in our age group, but they weren't interested. We went ahead because we didn't like what the future held if we stayed on our current path. Mostly younger people, those in their 30s to mid-40s, have decided to try the business. They're past the we've-got-it-all stage and realize they might not make all their dreams come true without something else."

Bob kept on working and and explaining the Amway Sales and Marketing Plan in the evenings and on the weekends. Their sponsors, Cliff and Cathy, lived in California so weren't able to be a geographically-close support system. The plan Bob shared with friends, neighbors and acquaintances explained how, through people inviting other people to join them in a business process, Amway home and cleaning products would be distributed and each person involved would make a profit on the wholesale and/or retail sales. The unique part of this system is that no one makes money without helping someone else. The more Bob trains and assists the people he has sponsored and the folks those people have sponsored, the more his business grows and the more he profits.

"I get really excited when I can assist someone in

his drive toward success," Bob said. "It's interesting that the more successful a person is when I show him this business, the more he or she is able to see the possibilities."

"I suggest they try it for even a year," Lois added. "It's such a small investment, what do they have to lose? If they attend the training events, use and sell the products and make the effort to share their business with others, they'll find that the program works."

The Hitzels are now at the "Ruby" level, but Bob was able to retire at 60 just as he'd dreamed because they had already become direct distributors. In 1989, Hitzel Enterprises grossed about $38,000, which isn't bad for a part-time business.

Both Bob and Lois work in their business with Bob doing most of the public speaking and presenting, while Lois minds the inventory and trains people how to order, stock, retail and promote the extensive line of household products, services and catalogues. According to Lois, she and Bob not only have a great business, but time to have fun together.

"We'd never have learned what we have about living a positive lifestyle if it hadn't been for the training we've received in this business of ours, Lois said. "We can travel, take the time to be 'real' grandparents and still build to our goal of a Diamond Distributorship."

The Hitzels feel that their age has been both an asset and a detriment.

"We didn't have to worry about babysitters and children's activities like the younger people have to," Lois said. "At our age, the freedom to come and go gave us a real advantage in the time area."

"But we had lost contact with many people we'd known in our kids' school and sport events," Bob added. "When we tried to contact them, many had moved or divorced or even died. We just had a lot more contacts when we were younger."

One thing that comes through loud and clear when Bob and Lois talk about their business is the joy they receive from helping others become successful. Since multi-level marketing is predicated upon the concept that you become successful when you help those you sponsor become successful, it becomes primarily a "people" business. Enthusiasm and excitement are contagious and necessary to build and keep the momentum rolling.

According to Bob and Lois Hitzel, "The friends we've made far exceed the value of any money that we've made, but that increased income is the frosting on the cake." And it's taking the worry out of their retirement years. As they say, "Anyone can do what we've done — and more."

DIRECT SALES

This country has seen direct sales people since the first peddler packed his sack of needles, thread, ribbons, lace and assorted gew-gaws and set out across the countryside, calling from house to house. Since he was often the only visitor to far-flung home-steads, all welcomed him.

Today's version might be selling anything from pots and pans to encyclopedias, make-up to brushes. Some well-known, but definitely not the only, names in the marketing area of direct home sales are Fuller Brush, Avon, World Book, Watkins and Mary Kay Beauty Products. All of these are reputable companies with good products from which one can purchase items without making a trip to the store.

The main difference between direct sales and multi-level marketing is how those who do the sell-ing obtain their products. With direct sales, the product comes from the parent company via mail or UPS to the person who ordered it, instead of being passed through the line of sponsorship. Bonuses are routed much the same, but keep in mind that each company has its own method of both distribution and payment.

Mary Kay Beauty Consultant
Virginia Marshall

Virginia Marshall represents the evolution of the peddler's pack idea into the modern age in Northglenn, Colorado. She sets up displays of Mary Kay Beauty Products in her motor home and parks at office buildings to provide on-site skin care for working women during their lunch hour. She started with the place she used to work, then to her husband's workplace, and plans on expanding to local banks next.

Virginia started her association with Mary Kay Company two and a half years ago at age 60. She spent most of her working life teaching sixth graders, but after a move to Colorado, went into accounting for ten years. Both previous careers serve her well in her own business.

"I've always considered myself an educator, not a salesperson, and that's what I do now. I educate both men and women about skin care, and then demonstrate all our beauty products as people desire them. Mary Kay is first and foremost a skin-care company, one of the largest in the world today."

Virginia was invited into the business by her sister in Oregon; she now trains and encourages a unit of women she has started in the business. Each consultant is the owner of her own business and buys her products wholesale directly from the Mary Kay Company. A manager receives compensation from Mary Kay based on the sales of her personal organization.

From an initial order of $1,800, Virginia now stocks about $3,000 in products, so when a customer calls in a panic, Marshall has the mascara or blush or whatever is needed. One thing women in our society do *not* do without is their make-up.

Since the company operates on a money-back guarantee, women feel free to try new products, and Virginia arrives on a quarterly basis to keep them up to date.

Mary Kay Ash, owner and founder who started her company at age 55, believes consultants need recognition besides the money they are earning. Her pink Cadillacs as awards are now preceded by a red Pontiac GrandAm, but either way, the car shows its owner is working hard. Be it pins, jacket color, jewelry, trips or furs, Mary Kay consultants always have another achievement level to look forward to. The enthusiasm the process has created has spurred the company and its thousands of consultants to phenomenal financial growth.

Mary Kay is known world-wide for her methods of leadership and business concepts. The company she founded is a new Horatio Alger story, but with a woman at the core.

Virginia Marshall believes strongly that with training and encouragement, anyone can build this business.

"I learned that my business works best when I do something for it every day. I love to garden. I tried gardening one week and Mary Kay the next, but that wasn't effective. Now I let my husband do the garden and I concentrate on my beauty business."

Last year the business grossed about $7,000 for an average of less than ten hours a week. That is not enough to support herself, but Virginia is planning to expand her customer base from about 150 to 300 and add more consultants to her unit. Her husband's heart attack slowed her efforts for several months or she would have already been driving that sporty red car.

"I think my girls need the example as much as I want the car," she said. "That's the best way to teach, by example."

In addition to the promotions offered through the company, Virginia has devised sales promotions of her own. Sometimes when she sets up her motor home display, she serves lunch so her customers can eat and buy, and then dash back to work. Each quarter the company sends out a flier with new products, up-to-date information and specials. Virginia sends this promo piece to her clients and announces when the beauty van will come to call. Spring of '90 was the fourth circuit for this venture and Virginia says she is constantly improving on her service. One goal now is to devise a display system that she will not have to take down every time she moves the motor home.

Virginia has taken an ancient idea and given it a modern twist with Mary Kay products in a Beauty Mobile. That twist and following the well-devised plan of action from Mary Kay headquarters is turning Virginia's supposedly slowing-down retirement years into growing and exciting years.

REAL ESTATE

Selling real estate is an art in itself and could be defined as both service and sales. Instead of delivering the product directly to the client, the broker or agent brings the client to his new home, commercial property or, as in the case of Maurice Diette in Chapter 10, the client's new business.

Don Stewart

Don Stewart's only been in the real estate business for a few months, but he already knows the heady feeling of listing a new property and closing the sale on others. He works out of an established office but as an independent contractor, so he is in business for himself, "one that I thought about doing 25 years ago," he said.

Instead he built a career promoting and marketing commodities for farm organizations such as the Potato Growers in Washington and Idaho, Washington State Fruit Commission, The Apple Commission and even the Hawaiian Papaya Growers. All this was on a free-lance basis and covered many other small organizations across the country.

"I had in-store demos in about every grocery chain across the country to promote papayas," Don said. "This new fruit soon became synonymous with Hawaii, just like pineapple is."

Don finally tired of all the traveling and he and wife Kay settled on Bainbridge Island, Washington.

"Going back to school for my real estate license took real concentration," Stewart said. "I had no idea of all the legalities and procedures one had to learn. But I wanted to pass the test so I put in the effort. I'm a classic example that you *can* teach an old dog (I'm 67) new tricks."

Don agrees that he is fortunate to be in an area where houses are appreciating rapidly.

"Anything that is any good sells right away," he said. "We have so many people migrating to the Seattle area from California that the island is becoming a bedroom community for Seattle."

Stewart credits much of his quick success to Marie Gallager, owner/broker, who has become his mentor.

"She is so willing to teach anyone willing to learn that I feel privileged to be working with her. She's been in the area for years, so knows every person, road and piece of property. That's a major asset for a real estate broker."

While Don is an independent salesperson, by associating himself with an established office he has secretarial help when he needs it, a desk, phones and all the machines and supplies to make his work easier. For this he pays a percentage of his sales.

"But my time is mine," Don said. "I'm able to be flexible, but I'm available when a client needs assistance. That's the part I like the best, helping people find just the new home they are looking for, turning their dreams into reality.

"You have to like people to run a business of your own," he said. "No matter what kind of product or service you offer, you'll be involved with people somewhere in the process.

"Start small but dream big," he advised. "Don't borrow and be grateful if you have a pension or a working spouse to help you through the lean times at the beginning. But whatever you have to do, being your own boss is worth the effort."

HOME PARTY SALES

Back when that peddler was first plying his wares, he probably found that when several people were gathered together, he could give one demonstration and sell plenty of merchandise in a shorter period of time. Maybe he learned that if he entertained them, made it more of a social occasion, his customers bought more.

You can purchase nearly anything at a home party these days: crystal, jewelry, makeup, toys, clothing, home interior decorations, home maintenance, plants, and more.

The hostess always earns a nice gift or dollars to be used in purchasing things for herself as a reward for inviting her friends to her home. She also collects the payments for orders and sees that her guests receive what they purchased. The guests are frequently offered special prices on their purchases, and all have a good time.

The business owner who gives the party makes from 35 to 50 percent profit from a percentage of the sales. Her promotional expenses, such as advertising and hostess gifts, come out of her profits and it is her responsibility to deliver the party order to the hostess.

Go-Getters Tupperware
Harriett Glandon

If a passionate love of people is the number one criterion for success as a home-party salesperson, Harriett Glandon would be right up at the top. And she was. For nine years, five of them as a manager driving the blue station wagon awarded her by Tupperware, International.

She got into Tupperware because of her big heart. She hosted a party and the dealer needed one more recruit to earn a mink jacket. Harriett thought she'd try the business for just six months, but by the end of that time she was having so much fun she kept on.

Tupperware is the patented brand name for plastic housewares, renowned for their air-tight seals, and sold only at home parties. Other companies have used Tupperware's system for retailing their own products.

Harriett knew that service was the key, that and giving a fun party. She led games and gave door prizes. She taught new uses for Tupperware pieces women already owned and introduced new items. Tupperware is always refining, improving and adding to its line, usually with special promotions to introduce a new piece.

Harriett's goal was always to make sure that her hostess earned the gift she wanted and had enough bookings (future parties hosted by one of the guests) to support the sales. The value of hostess gifts is always based upon the amount of sales plus the number of bookings. Outside sales and number of attendees adds to the total also.

"One time I really blew the warehouse away with my order," she said. "I'd given a party for a former hostess who ordered a new Fix-and-Mix bowl since she would be demonstrating bread baking at a local department store. Now, anyone who's ever baked bread using a Fix-and-Mix knows that sealing the dough in the bowl and placing the container in hot water saves about an hour and a half of rising time. When the seal pops, the dough is ready for forming.

"My hostess called me after her demonstration. 'Have you turned in your order yet?' she asked. When I told her no, she ordered nineteen more bowls. Her students had been that impressed. The next week after her demo, she ordered 10 more. If the warehouse had given awards for multi-sales of a single item, I'd have gotten it," Harriett said. "Times like that made the business fun for me."

She said she gave her biggest party the night she was home sick in bed. Husband Francis filled in with the hostess's approval and charmed the ladies into buying even more than usual. He often went along on evening parties to help with the set-up, the order-taking and hauling all the demo equipment back out to the car, so he knew the procedures well. One time he spent an afternoon babysitting all the guests' children out in the hostess' back yard. Some people will go to any lengths to give good care to their customers. Harriett and Frances live by the credo, "whatever it takes, do it." You can't go wrong with that kind of an attitude.

Harriett treated her recruits with the same loving care, keeping a large inventory on hand in case someone messed up an order or forgot something. Through the years additional shelves filled their garage, stacked high with Tupperware.

The business benefitted them at tax time too, since the U.S. tax structure is designed to assist the small business person, especially those home-based. And the Glandons didn't need to purchase a new car for those five years she was a manager.

While some distributors have been in the business for 25 to 35 years, Harriett chose to retire so she and Francis could travel to visit their far-flung family, without worrying about customer orders and party dates.

"This is a great business for older people," Harriett said. "It gets you out and interacting with lots of different people, which helps keep you young. While it's possible to support yourself through this business, it's ideal for those who want to add to a pension. You can pretty much set your own hours, working as much or little as you like. While it may be a drawback for some, much of your business will be in the evening. For us it wasn't a problem because Francis and I enjoyed those evenings together. If you love people, which you must to do a party-plan well, you'll have a great time. Everyone's in a party spirit, laughing and buying and just having a good time. You come away tired but knowing that you added a bit of joy to someone's life. And life without laughter isn't much living at all."

MAIL ORDER

Customers have been ordering purchases through the mail since Sears and Roebuck first introduced their catalogue many long years ago. That "wish book" became the granddaddy of a mail order dynasty that now sells everything under the sun, all delivered right to your door. Catalogues have proliferated in the last few years as more women work outside the home and have fewer hours to shop.

Today, more books and tapes are sold through mail order than any other item. Book clubs abound, with the major ones advertised in Sunday supplements, magazines and on television. But anything can and is being marketed by mail order today. All you need to begin this type of enterprise are products, a catalogue and a mailing list.

Co-operative Authors Marketing Service (CAMS)
Kay Stewart

CAMS, dreamed up by a group of five women authors at a writing conference, seeks to fill a niche in the catalogue marketing scheme. CAMS bills itself as "the good reading specialists," created to distribute good books beyond the usual bookstore outlets.

Kay Stewart, the marketing director for CAMS, is one of the original five women, all of whom divide up the duties of this growing organization. As a published author, Kay found the same frustrations as many other authors: haphazard and/or short-term marketing, especially for fiction.

The five sought to remedy this marketing void by inviting fiction authors, since expanded to include non-fiction, to join and use CAMS as an alternate avenue for selling their books. The CAMS quarterly catalogue is mailed to schools, churches and public libraries plus about 8,000 individuals, mainly on the West Coast.

Operating capital came from the sale of memberships, some venture capital from individuals and soon from the sale of books. The organization now lists about 75 authors and over 600 titles. Gross for the first full year of sales ran just over $39,000.

"That was pretty amazing to us, considering the shoestring we started with," Kay said. "We didn't get the venture capital we'd expected, so we just took one step at a time."

During the months of planning, the group decided that an S corporation would be the most practical, so the forms were drawn up and the designation applied for. They considered a not-for-profit corporation, but see their business as a money-maker someday in the future.

"After all," Kay said, "why brand our baby as a failure from the beginning? Down the road we may even become a publishing house, at least for our own books. We're working awfully hard to make CAMS make money."

Since this was to be a mail-order company, finding mailing lists was a priority. Each member brought her personal list and the original twelve authors invited to take part contributed theirs. They bought some lists, borrowed others, and constantly add to the current lists through trade-shows, conferences and those who order from the catalogue. Names are dropped after several mailings with no response.

The first catalogue mailed out touted the 100 books of the twelve authors, including the five board members. An accompanying letter invited authors to join the organization at several different fee levels or to invest in the corporation.

Kay took a class offered by the post office on metered mailings so they understood all the ins and outs of bulk mailings; how to sort according to zip code, how to weigh and wrap articles to be shipped and how to use the postal service most efficiently.

She also shopped around to find the best prices on shipping materials such as mailing envelopes, boxes and stuffing. They were quickly able to buy enough in bulk to deal directly with manufacturers and thus save money.

CAMS orders books directly from publishers to get

the best discount, which will improve as they are able to purchase more copies of each title at a time. They then fill the mail orders, which now amount to about 50 percent of the revenue.

The second avenue of marketing is more seasonal. CAMS sets up booths at school book fairs, association meetings such as The Librarians Association, writing workshops, education conferences, anywhere they can book one of their authors as speaker, conventions and seminars. They've traveled to Anaheim and Phoenix although most of their displays are in Washington and Oregon.

Books sell best at the booth when authors are available to autograph and promote their own titles, but even without authors, this side of the business is growing too. The best sales so far have been $949.00 in an hour and a half at a local school. One book fair grossed $1900, $400 of which went back to the school library in the form of books. CAMS already has received invitations to do more shows and fairs in the year ahead.

"I think our personal touch is one reason for our success with both the catalogue line and the booths," Kay said. "We order special inventory for Young Author workshops or bring our line to out-of-the-way locales. We go where we are invited, even though that first visit might not promise a large sale."

The newsprint catalogue grows with each issue. Whimsical artwork and book jacket reproductions draw attention to the different divisions. There are adventures, historicals, mysteries, romances, picture books, early readers, writing books, devotionals and classics. The books are for all ages and tastes with nary a story anyone would blush to read or be seen reading, even by their grandmother.

The women drew no salaries until May 1990 because they kept plowing all the profits back into inventory. Their May 1990 figures showed an inventory of $45,000 and $13,600 in profits for the year-to-date. Their income changed from 22% from sales to 66% from '88 to '89. The remainder of the income came from memberships.

By keeping careful books and tracking all their sales, they are able to look back and know exactly where they've been. Thus they can predict their probable growth for the years ahead.

That growth includes a wish list, the first item being office help so the writers can have more time to write. Since everything is paid for, some of their profits will go the way of an extra hand.

Kay advises anyone who markets a product to make sure you develop alternate ways to sell your goods.

"There are always going to be lulls in your sales, either seasonal or cyclical, so prepare new, creative ways to get yourself before the public." Right now she's thinking of a home party plan, but whatever avenue Kay or her cohorts dream up, CAMS will continue to sell good books to an ever-expanding customer base.

FOR ADDITIONAL INFORMATION

Even if you don't create a catalogue, don't rule out the possibility of sales by mail. Or could you sell your wares via home parties? Don't restrict yourself to the conventional. Be creative and keep an open mind.

Since this is a book on business and business *always* involves sales or selling, whether product or service, every example you read about can give you ideas for your own business. So read on.

GOOD READING

Starting and Operating a Home-Based Business, by David R. Eyler, John Wiley & Son, 1990 is strong on selecting personal computer hardware and software. He gives good information on direct mail and telemarketing.

Mary Kay, by Mary Kay Ash, Harper and Row, tells how and why she started her multi-million dollar cosmetic business. She tells an inspiring story.

Power Multi-Level Marketing by Mark Yarnell and Kevin B. McCommon, Austin, TX: Powerhouse Publications, 1988. Tells how to build a huge organization in MLM. The book is divided in two sections; one for those who want build fast, and the other for those who'd rather build slow and steady.

The Possible Dream by Paul Conn, Berkley Books, 1978. Tells the story of the Amway Corporation and the people who make it the "granddaddy" of multi-level marketing.

8

THE RETAIL STORE: BUILD IT — BUY IT — OR BECOME A FRANCHISEE

When a group of people settled in an area, that peddler we mentioned earlier often opened a store, stocked his shelves with everything a home or business could need, and waited for his customers to come to him. As a town grew up around his location, other more specialized shops opened.

Today we have stores at both ends of the spectrum. Huge one-stop supermarkets promise to make our shopping easy and small, very specialized stores and boutiques cater to individual tastes. Whichever you choose, depending upon your need of the moment, the retail store is here to stay and as adaptive as ever.

If owning a retail store is your dream, you can build the business from scratch, buy one already in existence, or purchase a franchise. Whichever you decide, location will play a prime roll in your degree of success. You've heard many business owners stress research, research, research. Taking the time

97

to check out your location will never be time wasted.

Research to see if there are others selling the same stock you are planning to sell. Does your town really need another shop selling widgets? Or perhaps that other store sells cheap widgets, but you plan to sell the "quality" model. Of course you've already checked to see if there are enough consumers with sufficient income to buy your highly desirable widgets.

Experts call research "finding your niche and marketing to it." You'll hear more about niche marketing in Chapter 16.

BUILD A BUSINESS

Let's look at two business owners who chose to build their businesses from the bottom up.

Roselle's Fabrics
Roselle Calihan

If you're a quilter in search of rainbow-hued fabrics, have bridesmaid and wedding dresses to sew for an up-coming wedding, or plan to make all your Christmas gifts this year, *Roselle's Fabrics* in Dodge City, Kansas is a good place to frequent. You'll find all your sewing needs there, including Viking Sewing machines, and if you're just beginning, an array of classes to hone your skills.

Roselle had been a seamstress most of her life between clothing four children and whipping up drapes, bedspreads and a quilt or two as the need arose. When she suddenly needed to make a living for herself, the first place she thought of was a fabric store. After four years as an employee, being trained in all phases of the business, Calihan figured she was ready to go it alone and moved to Dodge City.

She opened her own enterprise with a wide assortment of fabrics and notions in a remodeled 1,250 square foot ex-doughnut shop.

"My word," she said when thinking back, "I was scared to death that first buying trip. In fact, I was about ill at all the money I was spending."

Her daughter, the only full-time employee at the time, helped with displays, sewed sample garments and taught classes. Roselle soon found that quilting supplies and fabrics and trims for wedding finery were in the most demand, so as she reordered, she focused more of her inventory in those areas.

"I'm not ordering any more wool at all," she said. She also stays away from craft kits and supplies, decorator and upholstery fabrics.

Three and a half years later Roselle moved to a larger space in the basement of the local mall and outgrew that. In the fall of '89, she purchased the old Penney's building which she had remodeled into two sections, 2,500 square feet for her fabric store and the remainder for lease. Last year *Roselle's Fabrics* grossed $127,000 and carries an inventory around $100,000 at peak times.

"My last business class was bookkeeping in high school," Roselle said, "so in the very beginning I hired an accountant to set up my books and teach me the system. I do all the book work myself because that's the only way to keep track of your business. I *have* to know where the money is going."

Two years ago she invested in a Tandy computer, read the instructions and quickly became adept at keeping all her accounts, payroll, taxes and inventory in the computer.

"That machine sure has made my life easier," she said.

Roselle found that television ads at $9 per 30-second spot for a total of $180 per month, which cover a 100-mile radius, are her most effective advertising. You'll see her ads in the local newspaper, but she finds that most tourists locate her shop through the yellow pages.

"I never would have had time to run a business when I was younger," Calihan said, "what with raising a family and all. But I'm sure enjoying it now. I like the challenge, the creativity and my customers. They teach me all the time, always willing to share new patterns and ideas they've found. You get a group of women together who like to sew and you can hardly shut them up. My quilting classes are kind of like old-fashioned sewing bees."

Roselle tells new business owners to watch their pennies. "Your business can grow or be lost on the smallest things. And other than that, just do it. If I could manage to build a business like this, scared as I was at first, anyone can do it."

Trail's End Feed Store
Earl Crisp

When a man's been in the feed and grain industry all his life, you'd think he'd like to do something different for a business of his own. But not Earl Crisp.

Earl opened *Trail's End Feed Store* to distribute Purina feeds. He and his son, the only employee, haul bulk and sacked feed into Dodge City, and then deliver orders to their customers. Most of their business is in pre-mixed, bulk feed for the surrounding cattle ranches.

In the seven years since they opened the doors, they've seen good seasons and bad.

"The drought continues," Earl said, "so the farmers end up feeding more grain. A lot of them sold off part of their herds because there's not enough hay and pasture."

Crisp hasn't had to do many promotions or much advertising. In the summer, *Trail's End* has "dog-dipping-days" when the community can bring in their dogs to be dipped for fleas and ticks. Other than that, new customers come because of word of mouth or because Earl makes a personal call and invites their business. He makes sure he does the calling on a regular basis, and includes his steady customers too. Customer service is obviously the name of the game for Earl.

One day he had a woman phone for information.

"Do you have anything for my kids?" she asked.

"Well, that depends," Earl responded. "Are they

rug rats or drape apes? Because we have rat control pellets or monkey chow."

The silence on the line stretched until the woman laughed and said, "No, this is for my young goats."

"I was afraid she was upset," Earl said, "but half an hour later she was still laughing when she came in to pick up the goat chow for her 'kids'. She's turned into a real good customer and we all laugh about that conversation. Having fun like that is all part of good customer relations and one reason I like my business.

"I make sure I live up to my word, too. If I say we'll be there at a certain time, we're there. Our feed's good quality and folks around here trust us. That's the only way to build a solid business."

BUY AN EXISTING BUSINESS

The next two businesses are as different as pears and pomegranates. One moved stock to a new location and the other increased the market value of an existing store, but both of them had prime locations.

Roots — An Antique Store
Louise Perkin Byer

"I first worked for a friend who asked me to clerk in her antique store," Louise said. "But when she begged me to stay but couldn't find the money to pay me, I knew it was time to leave. In that apprenticeship I'd gotten a taste of the business and I liked it."

So when a friend offered her free rent for one-third of a building on a main highway near Dodge City, and a parcel of goods became available, Byer took the plunge. She invested $5,000 in a motley collection of goods and was in business.

"I checked out the antique furniture to make sure my investment was sound and groaned at the miscellaneous goods stacked in boxes. Moving all that stuff to the new location took a month. Thank God for good friends. The move almost wore out both my friends and my back, but we did it."

April 1 marked a day of celebration when Louise opened the doors to her new enterprise. Dealers, tourists, locals, all beat a path to her door, bought and returned. By October of that year, she had doubled her inventory, using cash generated by the business, which grossed $13,000 in the first year.

"I like to refinish furniture," Louise said. "A piece all restored and beautiful sells immediately. Folks just can't buy modern furniture with the quality of wood and construction of the old. I love the satiny feeling of oak, the furniture of the common people, when all the finish is stripped away and the wood is ready to varnish or oil again."

Pricing her inventory was a problem at first, but experience is a good teacher and Louise has never been afraid to ask questions, both of her customers and other dealers who make her place a regular stop.

"Tourists from California think my prices are pretty

low," she said. "But I have to take into account the area where I live. Here in rural Kansas prices are different than in the big cities."

Louise had retired from the civil service, and wanting something different, joined the Peace Corps and spent two years in Ecuador.

"When I came back, I knew I needed more income, so I kind of just fell into this business and love it.

"I don't know how I'd manage if I had any loans against my business," Louise said. "Worrying about the day-to-day stuff is bad enough. There are three businesses in our building, a gift store and another antique store, so we help each other out. I buy a lot of my inventory at auctions but people bringing things by is my best way to obtain new merchandise."

Last year Louise successfully placed fliers in hotels and motels around the area, so this year her artist daughter is creating a classier but still homey flier with which to do the same.

Byer has appeared on local television programs, one time to talk about her Peace Corps experience. Any appearance is wonderful free advertising.

"Little by little my name is getting known. I'm campaign manager for the man who owns the building in his bid for a local county office, and that gets my name out again."

They have signs on the building, and the three business owners are looking into approach signs to encourage the drive-by traffic to become stop-in customers.

"I like the freedom to use my own imagination. This is a great way to meet people. Some of my repeat customers will say, 'We were here last summer. Do you remember me?' And usually I do, either because of something they said or what they bought.

"I really don't think of my age at all," Louise said. "I guess it's an advantage because of all I've learned through the years, mostly about people. I look at myself as a smart 22.

"I'd tell people not to go into debt. It would be terrible to work this hard and not make it. I'm fortunate that a friend of mine is a good bookkeeper and keeps after me. Writing things down is so important."

"I've been fortunate in my friends who are always there to help me," Louise said. "That's what life is all about, family and friends, and if you can run a business and make a little money, you've got the best of everything."

Glandon's Shoprite
Francis and Harriett Glandon

Francis had been a meat cutter all his life with a dream of someday owning his own store. The chance to buy a local, run-down market came when he was 54. He invested his retirement from the meat cutter's union and with the advice and support of the West Coast Grocery Co., soon built the $14,000 inventory up to $32,000; within a couple of years, he purchased the building.

"We were doing three and a half times the volume when we sold compared to how we started. In the grocery business, if you can turn your inventory over in a month, you're doing well. We were turning ours over fifteen times a year," Glandon said.

"As our business grew and we got to know our neighbors, I appreciated the people around us," he said. "I knew we were more than just a business in the community. I hired local kids as box boys and called parents on some shoplifters. We received a great deal of pleasure watching some of those kids grow up, knowing we played a part in the process."

The Glandons felt those were good years and recommend owning your own business to anyone.

"You have to look at things realistically," he said. "You'll always have some difficulties to work through, but the effort is worth it in the long run. We had a good time with our business and that's important."

BUY A FRANCHISE

Nearly every business magazine you read applauds franchising as *the* way to open a business today. Articles frequently list the most promising franchises, and if you don't believe the articles, the ads will overwhelm you. You can buy franchises that are in business to clean carpets, cars, houses, offices, yards, windows and pets. Anything edible is sold through franchises, especially fast food. You can buy a school or a printing shop, repair cars, sell tires or real estate. You can buy clothing or auto parts stores, or a fitness center to fix up out-of-shape bodies by working out on the machines, which of course will go along with a new eating program, also a franchise.

"Today, franchising is a multi-billion-dollar industry, ringing up nearly $600 billion in sales annually and accounting for one-third of all the consumer purchases made in this country."
(Entrepreneur, April, 1990)

When you buy a franchise, you purchase the name, the product and the parent company's assistance in locating and developing a site, setting up the business, training you and your staff and giving on-going support.

For this you pay an agreed-upon purchase price and a percentage of your monthly profit. As John Walsh says in the following interview, research the various franchises carefully. All franchises are *not* created equal, no matter what their hype says.

Everything Yogurt
John G. Walsh

John Walsh chose a franchise business because, "I didn't know anything about running a business of my own. I'd been on the New York police force for 25 years until an injury forced me to leave. There

I was with a pension, a disability and the rest of my life to live."

The Walshs moved to San Antonio, where his wife had grown up, and John began exploring business concepts. He checked out Burger King, Sparks Auto Tune-up and Dunkin' Doughnuts, thinking that he wanted the expert backing of a franchiser. An ad in the paper for *Everything Yogurt* led him to his eventual enterprise.

"I really checked them out," John said. "I toured the New York locations and talked to the owners of *EY* franchises all over the country. Most of the responses were favorable. In that search I met a man who knew people I knew and we hit it off. He was really up front with me and answered all the questions I bombarded him with."

John bought the first franchise for $25,000 with a total investment of about $210,000 for site development, equipment, fixtures and supplies. He agreed to pay the parent company five percent of the net per month and a one-half percent advertising fee.

"Headquarters sent five people down here for seven days with two of them remaining another week. They taught us everything; from the book work to making shakes, cash register to cleaning, food preparation to filling and running the machines. Talk about thorough! They promised me if I needed them again, they'd be on the plane immediately. Instead I called them at least once a day for three months. This company gives *good* direction, it doesn't just sell franchises."

And it worked. John credits much of the success to the *EY* design of two restaurants in one. One side is *Everything Bananas* which serves frozen fruit drinks, lemonade, pretzels. The *Everything Yogurt* side serves yogurt, pita sandwiches, quiche and salads. The two share a kitchen.

"Besides, with this company you can be flexible," John said. "They suggest but don't insist. For instance, I sell Danishes in the morning. We're located right in the middle of the business district, so coffee and Danish go well. They said 'fine.' I appreciate that."

John purchased a second franchise in a suburban mall, a year after the first. His 26-year-old son runs one and his wife the other. Both loans are half paid off and the Walshs could live on the business income if they needed to. They're thinking of opening two more locations in the next couple of years.

"Opry Land is coming to town and a new sports center going up, so maybe I'll try to locate near them. But I'm in no hurry."

John had a good management background from the police force, so finds little difficulty in keeping his employees happy. The kids bring their friends and relatives in to get jobs, which is about the highest accolade possible.

"I treat my staff with respect," John said, "and make sure my managers are trained to keep the workplace pleasant. It's hard work, so the kids get regular raises if they put out the effort. Some of those who've been here awhile have gone from $3.50 up to $5 an hour. We don't have much trouble finding employees because the economy is slow right now."

John advises those looking into any kind of business to do their homework up front.

"Really dig into the idea. I asked other owners if they'd do it again. Check out the franchise company. Are they living up to all their promises? And really investigate the location. While the mall was under construction I sat out by the street and counted the people walking by. I watched where and what they ate. By the end of that time, I was certain my location was perfect."

Everything Yogurt has been good to John Walsh and he's been good for the company, consistently running in the top five percent of the 200 stores across the country. He didn't try to re-invent the wheel, he did what the trainers told him — and it worked.

Mr. Movies
Helen Russell

When two women get it into their heads that they *will* open a business together, they don't let problems like being jerked around by a restaurant franchise get in their way. Helen Russell and Jacki Greski worked for the county welfare system. While they weren't near retirement, they could see age creeping up and that their pensions would not be sufficient to maintain the lifestyles they earned.

After extensive research they decided to pursue the franchise idea.

"We weren't business people so felt this way we would get the support and training we needed to make our business a success," Helen said. "We saw an ad in the paper for a steak house franchise. They gave us a lot of build-up; got us so enthused we set up an appointment at the bank.

"The man we'd been dealing with showed up totally unprepared, kind of shrugged and said, 'Gee, I didn't know you gals were all that serious.' Basically I'm glad we got out of that one. The franchise is sound, but the franchisor didn't come off too well. While I hate to think the fiasco might have been because we were two women, I'd have a hard time believing they'd treat a business*man* like that."

It was back to the research boards, sadder but wiser. The next ad they answered was for a video franchise and another total zip. Helen and Jacki began to wonder if they *really* wanted a franchise or not.

On a trip to the Twin Cities, the two women stopped at a *Mr. Movies* video store just to compare. The owner sent them over to headquarters with his blessing. The treatment they received erased the previous bad experiences, and armed with sample contracts, brochures and franchise information, the two headed back to Bemidji.

"They helped us find a location and fixtures, order the right movies, set up the display gondolas, deal with all the legal work. It cost about $120,000 to open the doors and we've now been open a year," Helen said.

The women brought their years of management skills into their business and soon decided that Jacki would manage the store during the day and Helen help out at night, since Jacki was more able to leave her former position. They hired extra help as needed, offering free movies to help offset the low pay scale.

Since there were already other video stores in town, the *Mr. Movie* owners came up with promotions to bring customers into the store. They offered two-for-one on some nights, coupons in the local paper, Super Saver Cards where you rent so many and get one free, and specials advertised on fliers distributed around town.

As their clientele developed they focused more on the type of movies requested so their reputation grew as a good place to frequent. They now carry about 2,500 titles and over 200 Nintendo games. Experience also taught them how many copies of a film to order and rent at prices running from $3 for a new release down to $1 for children's films.

With high overhead in their location, they didn't break even at six months as the parent company predicted. Although break-even happened within the year, they still find themselves plowing most of their profit back into the business.

"We're thinking of a second location, though," Helen said. "The profit margin is such that if we can find a good spot not too far away, two stores would be a wise move.

"We've learned that when you go into business you must be prepared for everything to go wrong that can go wrong. You've got to keep your sense of humor and *don't panic*. If you just keep on keeping on, things will turn around and one day you'll take a deep breath and admit, yeah, we did the right thing."

FOR ADDITIONAL INFORMATION

Check up on other franchises in this book: Wold with *Holiday Inns* in Chapter 17, Rheinhart who is turning *Retiree Skills* into a franchise in Chapter 10 and Lappert who is franchising his ice cream stores in Chapter 3.

The greatest benefit seems to be the support and advice available if you need it, as well being able to plug into national advertising and promotions.

GOOD READING

Wishcraft—How to Get What You Really Want, by
Barbara Sher, Ballantine, 1979. Helps you define your goals and create a network to support you. Some good hints to make change and progress easier.

9

THE WHYS HAVE IT: REASONS FOR CHOOSING A BUSINESS

Why the people you meet in this book chose the businesses they did varies about as much as the businesses themselves. Some followed a long-term dream, others fell into their enterprises, surprised because the timing seemed so right. Some researched many possibilities, others found their new endeavor a natural progression from their former occupations or because someone steered them in the new direction.

The following stories should answer some "why" questions.

THE PIGGYBACK CHOICE

Top Publishing and Printing
John Frank, Jr.

"I didn't plan to start a business of my own, I was literally booted into it," said John Frank, Jr. "I'd been in the banking and stockbroker business all my life, but three months short of my being vested for retirement benefits, the big boss came to me one day and said, 'Clean out your desk.' As of that minute I was on my own."

John didn't even consider another type of venture at that time. He explained the situation to his clients and at their request became a consultant for stock portfolio management. He'd been leaning in that direction already, but at the stock-brokerage he was expected to be strictly a salesperson, even as vice president of the local office. It wasn't too many months later that John called his former bosses back to say "thank you" for the favor they'd done him.

But within two years, John needed a bigger challenge. He had an excellent reputation with his clients. In fact, in the crash of '87, his accounts broke even or better. No one lost money.

"I was really proud of that," John said, "but I was restless. Telling people what to do with their money just wasn't enough anymore."

John did all his accounts on his computer and as he prepared reports, the Ventura program for desktop publishing offered him graphics and print enhancements. As he became proficient in the program, he branched out into some typesetting.

For awhile a quality copier filled the expanding company's needs, but John's need for more challenges triggered the next step: printing. John researched the idea for about a year, talking with both printers and companies that sold printing equipment.

In November of 1989 he took the giant step by investing $30,000 in printing equipment. He purchased a used AB Dick 60 Chaindrive printer and began experimenting. He'd asked so many questions and observed others in his year of research that . . .

"I just did it," he said. "I seem to have an affinity for printing, guess that's about the best way to explain my process. But it works for me."

As needed, he added a plate maker, then a folding machine, a quality cutter and most recently, a stapler, circa 1860.

"The equipment will last forever, if cared for properly," he said. "I just watch the ads and pick up new pieces through sales."

Piggy-backing this added venture on an established, solid reputation added to his rapid rate of success. The first loan was paid off within several months and he hasn't borrowed since.

John scouted all the local printing companies to make sure he could underprice them for the initial orders, knowing that service would be the deciding factor for *repeat* business. By doing the work himself he could keep the cost down and the quality up. There would be no work delivered with blurred print or lines, crooked layout or sloppy folding. And work-orders would *never* be late.

John advises others not to borrow: piggyback one business on another already successful one if you can, work fourteen hours a day, six and a half days a week and enjoy the challenges.

"I don't ever tell people that a business of your own is easy," he said. "All I know is that it's worth every effort. What I was forced to do at 48 and 50, I should have done at 38 and 40. But then, you're never too old to learn. Most of us don't make changes unless we're forced to, or the desire is so great we can't do anything else. That's what brought my printing business about."

A DREAM BASED ON PAST EXPERIENCE

Hardscrabble Crafts
Charles S. (Chuck) Bergen

"Bringing about change here in Vermont is kind of like trying to push a worm back in a hole," Chuck Bergen laughed. "I've been here eleven years now and I'm still a flatlander (someone from outside Vermont) to many people, but some have 'taken me in' (accepted me as part of the community). Still I wouldn't live anywhere else and I have met some terrific people."

Chuck Bergen retired from life as a graphic artist and owner of an advertising firm so he and his wife could move from Ohio to Bristol, Vermont to be closer to their grandchildren. The fact that they loved the area had some bearing on the move. His dream was to be a "real" artist, both creatively and as a business.

The first scenic drawings of New England he put on paper came nowhere near the photos he took or the visions in his head. Using varied sizes of technical drawing pens, he created line drawings with the look of etchings, but the final product took many stages and repeats before meeting his exacting standards.

"Most of them I just tossed," he said. "I'm working in an unforgiving medium — you don't erase, you pitch. I couldn't believe it took so much effort — but I won."

Getting the originals printed proved to be the next hurdle. No one in the area seemed to understand what Chuck wanted, even after he gave detailed explanations. And gave them again.

"About the only advantage I can see in living closer to the cities is having access to quality services like printing," Bergen said. He finally trained a local shop and produced note cards, post cards, gift enclosures and framable prints using the different Vermont and New England scenes. Lighthouses, animals, a round barn, distinctive houses, a covered bridge, all expressed the unique feeling of the countryside.

Bergen also draws a building upon request, charging anywhere from $200 to $400. The owner of the drawing can then use it any way he desires, usually for brochures or postcards for advertising.

In order to market his line, Bergen joined The Vermont Hand Crafters, a nonprofit organization which is the marketing medium for products handcrafted in Vermont. Membership is by juried invitation;

there are about 300 members. Articles are sold at special art and craft shows which bring in about $10,000 a week year-round, to be distributed to the participants.

Bergen says he spent so much time on the organization, especially the last year when he was president, that his own business suffered. But he felt it was worth the effort as he became well known and respected for his art work.

"I'm pretty particular about where I sell my card line," Bergen said. "The stores must offer a quality line of gifts and cards, with the stock well presented. If things are just jumbled together, my things, and most of the rest of the inventory, won't sell. Also the outlets can't be too close together for competition. My things really do well at the Trapp Family Lodge, for which I've produced drawings as souvenir items."

Chuck now has an agent who had to be educated in Bergen's principles to market his card line well. So far all outlets are in Vermont, but that can change as Bergen's drawings are of scenes in New Hampshire and Massachusetts, too.

While Chuck doesn't plan on getting rich in this field, the $14,000 he made in his best year contributed to a comfortable lifestyle.

He sees his age of 65 as an asset in his business venture. "I brought in all my past experiences and training," he said, "the accumulation of years. I'm more mellow now, more tolerant and I can take the time to enjoy the people, the process and the area itself."

His advice to other would-be business owners is to research, research, research. Start with the phone book, go to the library, ask other business people, talk to business organizations like the chamber of commerce, and the SBA, to see if there is a need in your area for the business you want to begin.

"Most businesses that I've seen fail are because someone said 'Gee, I'd like to open a craft shop,' for an example, and never researched the location, the need or how to run a business."

Bergen recommends building a good relationship with the research librarian at your local library. She will be a tremendous help in locating information for you if you just tell her what you have in mind. Then read, read, read.

"I'm pretty much self-educated," Chuck said. "You can learn about anything through books and magazines; *then* ask questions. Remember too, that if your library doesn't have the materials you need, inter-library loans can put any publication at your fingertips.

"If you're concerned about your lack of knowledge of how the library works, that is, card systems, computers, microfiche, don't worry. That wonderful librarian will train you. Sometimes it's a good idea to make an appointment with her, if you need a lot of help. But don't be embarrassed; libraries have changed and expanded since you went to school.

And with new equipment, they're changing more all the time.

"I'd like to sell my business," Chuck said, "and go into painting. After all, I'm supposed to be retired and have time to do what I wish. Any buyers out there?"

BECAUSE THE NEED IS SO GREAT

Divorce Action Self-Help Centers, Inc.
June B. Brown

"I'd been a paralegal for 20 years," June said, "working for attorneys and gaining experience. I realized that those who sought a divorce but had nothing to divide, or those on low income or welfare, couldn't afford an attorney. They didn't really need an attorney for advice; they just needed their paperwork filled out accurately and the filing done. I could do that."

She moonlighted in the business for a time, until at a friend's urging, she rented an office in Martinez, California. Since June already had a good reputation, lawyers and judges referred clients to her, and word of mouth quickly spread news of her service.

"Within four months, I had to hire part-time help," June said. "Some days I had clients waiting in line and out the door. I had so much work to do that I never had time to build the business properly."

It wasn't long before she expanded to Solano county, where again, she opened her office in the county seat, Fairfield.

"I make sure I'm within walking distance of the court house, both for my convenience and that of my clients."

June said she does more than fill out divorce papers, she's become somewhat of a counselor, referring clients to agencies that can help them with their problems of substance abuse, poverty and poor education.

"Some people look on self-help divorce as a depressing business, but I know I offer a necessary and beneficial service. And it's lucrative." Her business grossed $80,000 last year.

June admits that her biggest problem is interviewing and hiring competent help. Because of a rash of bad experiences, she is now using temporary help through an agency and is pleased with the quality of work being done.

"I'd suggest that anyone thinking of a business interview the professional help they need, such as attorneys, bookkeepers, CPAs, besides those they need to hire for their staff. Ask for references and check those out. I would have saved myself hours of agony and untold dollars if I had followed this belated advice. Now I've hired a business consultant to advise me on not only getting out of the messes I've experienced but to help me proceed in an orderly manner. My business has been successful in spite of me, so what will happen when I'm following appropriate procedures? I'm looking forward to the next months and years.

"If you put your clients first," she continued, "the dollars will follow. I'm sometimes accused of being a 'bleeding heart,' but when you are dealing with hurting people, you have to take time to listen. As a paralegal, I can't offer advice, that's an attorney's job, but I can offer an ear and a hug when needed. Guess you could call my listening time my advertising budget. When a woman with a blackened eye sits in front of my desk twisting her fingers in her lap, barely able to look me in the eye, and whispers, 'My friend said you could help better than anyone,' I know I'm in the right business."

FOR ADDITIONAL INFORMATION

All the people in this book can offer you additional information as to the "why" they chose their particular businesses. As you follow Bergen's advice and do your research, don't overlook any ideas, no matter how inappropriate they may seem at the time. They may be an integral part of a picture that you are putting together piece by piece, so write *everything* down and file it for future reference.

GOOD READING

Success Magazine, 342 Madison Ave., New York, NY
10173, keeps you up-to-date on new ideas, business successes and products. Informative articles.
Founded by W. Clement Stone. Some magazine racks carry this magazine.

10

SENIORS SERVING; SERVING SENIORS

By the year 2020, the U.S. Census Bureau says that nearly one-third of the U.S. population will be 55 and over. Those who think of beginning a business would do well to look into providing products or services for this segment of our population, which controls nearly half the discretionary income in America.

Ken Dychtwald, founder of Age Wave, Inc. in Emeryville, California, consults with established businesses on selling to this mature population, but he also advises business owners who are developing businesses to create products or services for this market.

"Get your business going now, before the wave crests," he advises. "This is a marketing field that will only continue to grow."

The following two businesses focus the spotlight on the over-50 population, one hiring seniors and the other making them beautiful.

Retiree Skills, Inc.
Robert Rheinhart

Bob Rheinhart made a career out of starting businesses, first an insurance company, second an investments firm, and then he retired. Bob moved to Arizona where he could play as much golf as he'd always dreamed of and had never taken time for. He found plenty of partners, shot a multitude of greens, and got bored.

"You can only shoot so much golf," he finally admitted. And he hit his fill of the game after only three years.

On the fairways and in the pro shops he heard a recurring song of complaint from his fellow retired folk, most of them older than he. They either didn't have enough to do or if they had plenty they'd like to do, they didn't have the money to do it with.

From research Bob found that 35 percent of all retirees would rather be working and that 50,000 seniors had migrated to the Phoenix area. He saw this group as a tremendous, untapped labor pool. Next he contacted local businesses to make sure there were opportunities for skilled, dependable, part-time workers. Bob found that in these local employers' minds, only age was the barrier.

"I started advertising," Bob said, "for people with all kinds of skills, from office to custodial, engineering to education. I even found a clown. I advertised in both the local newspapers, a shopper newspaper, buses, taxis, radio. I told my seniors that the slogan for this enterprise was *From Inactivity to Productivity*. It's a simple statement and a simple concept, but it works.

"I beat the streets calling on businesses of every kind. I told the owners they couldn't lose. My bonded company would hire and pay the employees, pay the Social Security, unemployment, workman's comp and all other taxes. The employers would pay my company an agreed upon rate above and including the hourly wage. This rate differs according to job classification. The wage I pay the retirees begins at $4 an hour."

If that seems low, keep in mind that Social Security limits the amount of money retired people can make without penalty. Those from 65 to 70 can earn only $9,360 without being taxed about $1 for every $2 earned. After age 70 there are no restrictions. (This is true as this book goes to press. Check with your Social Security office for current information; announcement of change is made every November for the following year.)

Most people try to find work in other places first and only come to *Retiree Skills* when the age door has slammed in their faces too many times.

"When I go out to sell to the companies I tell them they'll have a stable, dependable work force on a part-time basis. And that's only a portion of the bargain they get," according to Rheinhart. "Aside from the seniors' very marketable skills, their old-fashioned work ethic is a far cry from what's fashionable with the younger crowd. My people understand the concept of service, that without service you have no repeat customers, no matter how good your product."

More than 300 local companies have used *Retiree Skills* employees and Rheinhart's company keeps an active file of 800 workers. Nearly 250 found work through *Retiree Skills* in 1988, and in the eleven years of the company's existence, it has made more than 2,500 placements, some of them permanent.

"We have such a tremendous variety of skills here," Bob said. "One day a woman from IBM Credit called me. She laughed when she said, 'I don't know if you can help me this time. I need a clown.' 'Don't laugh,' I told her. 'We have a clown, an experienced one.' Our clown made a whopping success of their company's family party."

Bob's unique and needed venture has received national publicity, leading him to the natural next step, franchising *Retiree Skills, Inc.* While he'd had the expertise to get his initial venture off the ground and flying, this time he hired a team of legal experts ("and paid them an exhorbitant price") to draft the program for franchising. The attorneys created all the legal documents and guidelines necessary while Bob wrote the training and operations manuals.

When those steps were completed, Rheinhart began a new round of advertising, this time searching for people who wanted to own a temporary skills company, employing only those over age 50.

The franchises, which are a real bargain for the new owners, have started in Phoenix and Las Vegas.

"The basic franchise fee is $15,000," Bob said. "Above that, prospects need $10,000 for operating capital and another $5,000 for the office and miscellaneous expenses. We help set up their office, give them a week's training and coach them as the business grows. Their success depends upon how hard they want to work. I always tell them they need money to live on from another source until the business becomes profitable. Too many people start paying themselves large salaries right away and their business goes down the drain.

"I like everything I've ever done," Bob said. "But this better than all the others. I don't plan to retire. My goal is to live 'til I'm 98 and be shot to death by a jealous husband."

Bob says all his years of experience have contributed to his success and through franchising he can pass some of that wisdom along. He's not sure how to find women entrepreneurs yet, but since women manage 80 percent of the temporary services, a woman would be a natural purchaser of a *Retiree Skills* franchise.

Rheinhart suggests that people who dream of their own business take a good hard look at themselves. Can they actually do what they desire? Do they have the finances to carry through? Are they willing to work harder than any of their employees ever dream of?

"Survey your area first and make sure there's a need for your business," he said. "In the beginning I sent out 120 letters by direct mail and got over a 40 percent response. Professionals consider a mailing super successful with a five percent return. So I knew there was a niche out there for my idea. That's what it takes, knowing yourself, knowing your area and learning all you can about your kind of business."

The Color Works
Gloria M. Rickert

Gloria has been involved with color for 45 years. Six years ago she added a Mary Kay business to her already existing business, *The Color Works,* in Redding, California.

"I'd had another brand of beauty products before that," she said, "but Mary Kay offered so much more as a potential business, and its products and service are always reliable."

Gloria offers a wide range of services and products to help women become more confident and use their time and money to the best advantage through color analysis, personal image and investment dressing. Her clients can choose a full makeover session taking an hour and a half at a cost of $75 or pick and choose services according to her time and budget. The pick-and-choose plan can total $90.

A computer imaging program assists Gloria in

teaching each client how to dress for her personality and figure type; the client will see on the computer screen what she will look like with the changes. This even applies to appearance changes with weight loss.

"I love talking with my clients," Gloria said, "so I can learn about them, their personalities, their lifestyles and help them create the look that takes advantage of all their best characteristics and minimizes problem areas. Everyone feels better wearing the colors and styles that best suit them."

Gloria learned in-depth secrets of color from a doctor when she was in the hospital with a broken back.

"He not only told me that our internal organs have cool and warm tones according to our body chemistry, he showed me." Gloria attended several surgeries and was able to see the difference herself.

"You can never change who you are," she continued. "You just have to learn to make the best of who and what you are."

Many of Gloria's clients are in the over-50 group as these women re-enter the workplace or finally take time for themselves, now that the children are gone.

"We have many, many retired people settling here in Redding," Rickert said. "I've taken my seminars to senior centers, church groups and private parties. I love going to nursing homes. Nothing is more of a pick-me-up than a facial and some new makeup."

Gloria has remodeled a room in her home into her studio, including plenty of mirrors and good natural lighting. Here she does private make-overs, retails her Mary Kay products and displays her scarf and jewelry lines. By the time a client walks out the door she will have had a facial, chosen the proper makeup and learned to apply it, studied her figure and personality type to know what style clothes to wear, and been advised about her best colors so she always wears those suited for her. She'll have a booklet with fabric swatches in her colors so she can match garments in stores. She'll also have a workbook filled with her personal details to help her study further and keep her on track. She'll know more about purchasing new garments to coordinate with those she already has in her wardrobe and choose accessories to finish every outfit.

Gloria's motto is: "It doesn't take a million dollars to look like a million," and her goal is to put this motto to work for every woman who walks through her doors.

Her Mary Kay business is growing apace as she recruits new women into the Mary Kay concepts and teaches them how to build an effective business on a part-time basis. Gloria says she spends about 20 hours a week on her business and hopes her dealers will do the same.

"The rewards are there for anyone willing to put in the time and effort," Gloria said. "But you have to make that commitment. And that goes for any age. If you choose to be in business, you have to be committed to that business, but more so, you have to be committed to your customers. If your goal is to make their lives better, the money will follow."

FOR ADDITIONAL INFORMATION

Remember that any business will have the opportunity to serve people over 50, but keep your eyes open for needs generated mainly by this age group. Ask yourself what service or product *you* would like to improve your life. Then develop that idea and market it to those around you.

There will be increasing media coverage, product development and advertising focus for this age group as America continues to age, so keep your eyes and ears open. You never know when a good idea will pop up.

GOOD READING

The Power of Positive Thinking by Norman Vincent Peale, Prentice Hall, 1952.. Another book that should be read yearly. It will help you believe in yourself and change negative patterns of thinking so you *can* succeed.

Age Wave, by Ken Dychtwald, Ph.D., Tarcher Press, 1989. Predicts changes ahead as America ages. Good ideas and advice for business owners.

11

SCHOOL ISN'T THE ONLY PLACE TO GET AN EDUCATION

Your idea for a business has now solidified. You know *what* you want to do, but you're not certain *how*. You've been learning from other people's experiences and now we'll add another dimension: education and where to get it.

There are usually two kinds of advice given by educators: theoretical and practical. Most college classes deal in the former, but some community colleges offer classes taught by business people who are in the trenches. Adult education programs sometimes offer business-related courses, and many times you'll see ads in your local paper for seminars related to your field of interest and need.

I always advise would-be-writers to take classes only from teachers who are selling what they teach. I shy away from theory or creative writing because they don't deal with marketing, and as in any business, a good portion of your time goes into marketing — or you don't pay the rent. The following man found his expert and took the classes.

LEARN FROM CLASSES

Income Tax Preparer
Herbert W. Rosch

Some people just can't seem to retire. They try, but when a former client begs for help, they relent. When income tax season rolls around, Herb Rosch is like an old fire horse snorting and pawing at the sound of the fire bell. He can't seem to turn down a request from his faithful clients. He tried selling the business, but even that didn't work.

Herb started doing taxes part-time for H & R Block before he retired the first time. He took a beginner's tax course while he worked in the county welfare department and wrote tax returns in his spare time in Bemidji, Minnesota.

During his first retirement he built his tax business into a year-round concern, acting as both an accountant and a tax specialist. While he added computer skills to his business, his wife remained the typist.

"I was always careful to learn the latest tax laws," Rosch said, "but the last few years have been atrocious. I've had to go back to school each year to keep up, not just study the changes myself."

Rosch retired a second time, selling his thriving business to a CPA in the area with the understanding that Herb would work for the company during the tax season for the next three years. About the same time, his son was going into business doing accounting and taxes, so Herb helped him out. When the son went back to work for another company, Herb was left with the business.

"Please, Dad, don't advertise," pleaded the son. "Don't take on new clients." So Herb now takes care of only a few long-time clients because he knows their business better than anyone else.

Herb's advice for new business owners is, "Hire a good accountant. If you want to do your own books, have a qualified person set them up for you and train you properly. Don't scrimp in this area. Either method you use, make sure you work with someone you can trust to give you good advice.

"Have an expert do your taxes. The rules change too rapidly to try completing a business return yourself.

"Don't be afraid to ask questions. You own the business, you have to understand what's happening, where your money is going. And where it's coming from. Too many new business owners don't pay enough attention to the bottom line. Numbers never lie. And when you pay attention, they tell you the full story of your business."

LEARN BY SELF-STUDY: BOOKS

Many of the most successful business people claim to be self-educated: they learned from experience. However, you can also be self-educated by reading and studying on your own. The following business owner suggests self-study as a viable way to learn.

March Media, Inc.
Etta G. Wilson

Making your living as an editor in the publishing business is like playing an eternal and swiftly revolving game of Musical Chairs. And like that game, when your company cancels your chair, you're out. Instead of jumping back in the game with another chair-owner, Etta Wilson opted to pursue a dream, forming her own company: *March Media, Inc.*, in Brentwood, Tennessee.

With the growth of conglomerates in the publishing industry, editors must spend more and more time in meetings and have too little time left for developing manuscripts. Thus, a fairly new service has emerged, that of book packager — a composite of agent, editor, and production, but with no allegiance to a particular publishing house. There are over 300 book packagers across the country, whose services range from editing to printing.

"As a book packager, mainly of children's books," Etta said, "my work can begin with either a manuscript from an author, or a request from a publisher. Then I take the project through all the steps of writing, design, illustrating and up to camera-ready copy or in some instances, right through printing. It all depends upon what the publisher wants. Today when houses are so short of staff, my kind of business takes up the slack."

Like many other business developers, Etta drew on her years of past experience in the industry for contacts and skills. "I knew I had to begin right away," she said, "before all my contacts disappeared. This industry changes so rapidly that it would be easy to lose track of people or even companies."

Etta chose to continue her work with children's books (her last position was as a children's book editor) because of the impact good books can make on young people's lives.

"I see more adults reading children's books, too," she said. "Adults have always been the chief buyers of children's books but now, more than ever, they are reading and enjoying children's literature. It might be because of the tremendous surge in quality in this field now. Talented artists like Chris Van Arlsburg create stories and pictures that communicate to all ages. Or it may be that adults are trying to recapture some of the joys of childhood or even because of the lowering of the adult reading skill level. But I prefer to think it's because of the wonderful artists and authors."

Wilson sometimes acts as an agent, primarily in adult fiction or for books she just doesn't have time to package. Because of all of her activities, She is adding more staff to the part-time secretary she has now.

"I like being able to see a project through to completion," she said. "And managing the creative team is a deeply satisfying feeling."

One of the business skills that Etta had to learn by doing was pricing her services. She's in a field with a slim profit margin so pricing each step of the process is crucial but rarely cut and dried. There are numerous variables for each step; for example, paper: what weight, size, finish, availability. There are also the human variables, all the different people who will touch the project somewhere in the process. Once she's covered all the charges, Wilson must add a margin for overhead, expenses and extra for a cushion, just in case — all with a goal to build capital to take on the next project.

Etta says one business book was a tremendous resource; she went back to it again and again. Paul Hawken wrote *Growing a Business*, using his experiences with several businesses of his own. The book is highly readable (one needn't have a degree in business to understand and apply the basic principles Hawken teaches), and even entertaining.

"If you're going to start a business, it also helps if it is something you already know and want to do," Etta said. "My friends and contacts were invaluable in the beginning and still are. You must have a widespread network to assist you because your business may grow best in unexpected ways. Success to me comes from a combination of contacts, quality product and persistence. People out there have to know who you are and what you do. Press releases, trade shows, brochures, hours on the phone — all are part of promotion.

"Don't conclude that the professionals you need to help you — for instance, lawyers, CPAs and bankers — are always on your side. They're most often out to make money from your business, not just be of service. You must keep a careful eye on all aspects of your business. Find people you think you can trust and then learn as much of what they do as you can. That's just good business sense. Remember, it's your business."

Clearly, Etta Wilson didn't learn everything about business from a book. But the book gave her good advice and helped her learn from her other sources.

LEARN FROM SUCCESSFUL PEOPLE

One excellent way to get an education is by listening to other people in your industry. This is especially true if you're buying a franchise or opening a distributorship. The people above you are supposed to train you. It is to their benefit to do so. If you do well, they do well. Many of the businesses discussed in this book are based on that principle: If I help you get where you want to go, I will get where I want to go.

The next profile shows the validity of that principle.

Basement Waterproofing Nationwide-VT
Ernest and Ruth Ferguson

How does a couple who do *not* consider themselves business people go from zero to half a million dollars in business in four years? They do exactly as they're told in a franchise for waterproofing basements.

"My friend was the owner of the parent company for this type of franchise and when I told him I wanted the franchise for Vermont, he told me, 'You'll make it, Ernie, if you do exactly as I tell you. I know what works. You don't need to re-invent the wheel.' And that's exactly what we did," Ernest said. "We started four years ago with a Ford Tempo van and the equipment to begin production."

The Fergusons knew their product was needed. Basements frequently spring leaks and trenching around the walls to refinish the concrete or stone is prohibitively expensive. The sealant product from Montana (sodium bentonite, a volcanic mix, called an hydraulic clay in natural form) is liquified and pressure-pumped into the ground around the building. This compound follows the path of least resistance and hardens into a gel-like substance that creates an impenetrable seal against the wall. For new construction, the slurry is pumped into the tubes of flat cardboard and attached to the exterior of the basement wall. Either way, the customer has a dry basement, permanently.

The Fergusons advertise their product in an unusual way, mostly from their booth at home shows and fairs. They offer $400 off the price if someone will sign an order with them at the time. Each job is done on an estimate basis, dependent upon structure size, travel distance and type of soil surrounding the dwelling. The company does both residential and commercial property with the greater percentage of their business coming from residential.

Ernest says that keeping competent help is a big headache. He, like many other business owners, finds that his most dependable help is over 50.

"They believe in showing up when they say they will and doing the job right the first time," Ferguson said. "I hate nothing more than to have a customer call me, irate because she took time off from work to have her basement waterproofed and no one showed up. I switch them over to Ruth. She's much better at handling unhappy people than I am."

They've had one salesman since the beginning, but the Fergusons could use one or two more. Good sales people are hard to come by. Ernie explained selling in Vermont with this story:

"A man had a hefty load of logs down by the lake that he needed hauled up a steep road. He hitched a team of strong, young horses to the load and slapped the reins. They pulled the load across the flat but when it came to the hill, they slipped and slid and puffed to a stop.

"The man went up to the farmer at the top of the hill and told him the problem. 'Wait here,' the farmer said, and returned with an old, blind horse. 'Hook him up in place of those two.' Dumbfounded, the man did as he was told and the old horse dug in and hauled that load right to the top.

"'How could that be?' the man asked when he returned the old horse.

"'Well,' replied the farmer, 'he couldn't see how big the load was nor how steep the hill, so he just did his job.'

"Salesmen tell me they can't sell in Vermont, the economy is too bad or there are no houses left to do, but I must be like that old blind horse," Ernie said. "I find a customer or two whenever I go out calling." Ernie and Ruth are living examples of their advice to others. Learn all you can about the business, listen and do what you're told, and then go out and just do what needs to be done. Oh, and keep a good sense of humor along the way, especially about yourself. Then, maybe like the Fergusons, you'll be in the position of having a thriving business to sell, even if you're *not* a businessman.

LEARN FROM GOVERNMENTAL SOURCES
Small Business Administration (SBA)
Service Corps of Retired Executives
(SCORE)
Local Business Development Center

These three resources are all tied together and yet each offers different services. You can take classes from SBA at your local Business Development Center. These are usually listed in your local newspaper and well worth the time. Several business people in this book refer to the help they received from the SBA.

But the best way to begin is by calling and requesting that the *Small Business Start-Up Kit* be mailed to you. The packet includes information about SBA and its loans, brochures, and a directory of Business Development Publications and where to order them. You'll be impressed with the publications our government puts out. And most of them cost only 50¢ or $1. The kit also includes copies of some of those publications, lists of local offices, contact people for SCORE, forms to register for classes and dates offered. Read and study this information, and then call for an appointment.

This is where SCORE comes in. These retired executive volunteers bring all their years of experience to your conference. You can tell them what you're dreaming of and they'll ask you a myriad of questions, designed to help you see your idea more clearly. They'll help you see your strengths and weaknesses and will suggest your next step.

Jean Lamb tells about her experience with these helpful people.

Precious Pockets, Inc.
Bob and Jean Lamb

> *Jean once made a little lamb,*
> *Its fleece was white as snow.*

She named the lamb of real sheepskin, Winky, and sent him off to her homesick daughter away at college. The lamb was cuddly, huggable and had a pocket into which a special verse was tucked, composed and hand-lettered by this artistic mother.

The daughter wrote in her thank you note, "Winky

Lamb gives me the constant care from home that I need and when I hug him, he hugs me back."

The lamb and poem became the basis for a burgeoning business which includes five lambs of various sizes, a line of greeting cards and a family game. The motto for all is: *Pocket Fillers, the next best thing to a hug.* Jean says that after four years in the Kettering, Ohio business which is marketed via the U.S. Mail, book stores, a new sales representative and Jean herself, the company is in the black.

Jean has always been a creative person, but this is their first home-based, family-run business venture. The Lambs contacted the Dayton Small Business Development Center for advice, and SCORE members helped them set up a marketing plan, a business plan, and gave them other suggestions as needed.

At first Jean made all the critters herself, but as the business grew, she had to look outside for help. Before she could hire a seamstress, Jean did time and motion studies on each process since the extra help would be paid on a piece-work basis. The three smaller lambs are made from scraps of the larger, so time is the major factor. For example: Winky Supreme costs $10.50 to make, including time and materials, takes one hour and fifteen minutes to sew, and retails for $34.50. Her assistants take the materials home to produce the lambs on their own time. Jean, a stickler for perfection, trains her seamstresses in the most efficient methods.

The card line has expanded from two or three to 31 designs packed in sets of six, and can be ordered by six of one design or in mixed packages. Jean had five Christmas designs in '89 and, as in the other series, is adding more this year. The cards are simple line drawings, but the designs and messages tug at the heartstrings.

The newest addition to the Lamb industry will be several family games, still in the brainstorming stage.

Locating a printer that gives quality work and clear reproduction, all at a reasonable price, came about through trial and error. Folding seemed to be especially difficult.

"The edges would be off by as much as a quarter of an inch," Jean said. The Lambs went through four printers before they found the one they are happy with now. "We're fussy," she said. But it takes that intense attention to detail to create a quality product.

Finding a source for the gray and white sherpa wool they use is an on-going problem, as the quality changes with shipments. Right now they order from a house in Baltimore. It's the little things Jean does that help set her business apart. For instance, the labels of the lambs say "filled with 100 percent polyester and love," and a verse is on the backs of the cards too, not just the front and inside.

"We follow where the lambs have led us," Jean said. "As you can see we are a small business. However, our goals are not in terms of dollar profits. If the 595 lambs last year filled that many 'pockets' plus the 7,779 cards, that's a total of 8,374 'pockets' that, just maybe, were a bit fuller because of our business. It looks like that total will be much higher in '90. It's hard to explain this to most people, because ours is a very dollar-oriented society. But our reward comes in having the Dayton Ronald McDonald House give Woolies and cards to their families who stay with them, in hearing about the churches who give Petites to all of their new members, or in hearing about how Suzanne Jackson uses our lambs to help her cancer patients cope. And knowing that Dartmouth Children's Psychiatric Hospital will be soon using lambs in their therapy with the children."

When you pick up a *Precious Pocket* lamb or read a card, you can't help smiling and feeling the hug that is sent with each message, which is exactly what Jean Lamb has in mind.

LEARN FROM YOUR LOCAL OR STATE CHAMBER OF COMMERCE

When I asked the Walnut Creek Chamber of Commerce for a copy of their Business Start-Up Kit, they asked me if it was for a sole proprietorship/partnership or a corporation, since the kit is different for each. The charge was $25 plus tax and a gold mine just in the time saved by not having to run down all the forms.

146

The SBA packet told me what forms I'd need in my state, but this kit included all the forms and instructions, and divided the sections by immediate, monthly, quarterly and yearly so I was prepared for the first year, all the way through final taxes.

The instructions recommended I ask for professional help, such as a CPA and attorney, rather than depending completely upon myself and my reading skills. But I was amazed at the wealth of information contained in the packet, bound in a tablet so I wouldn't get the forms out of order.

The chamber also offered business seminars covering a broad range of topics, for both its members and the general public. Most people associate chambers of commerce with their monthly mixers, but new and prospective business owners will find their local chamber of commerce a valuable resource in terms of information, not only networking. (We'll talk about the value of networking in Chapter 16.)

GOOD READING

Jerry Jinnett and Linda Pinson in Fullerton, California teach business classes. Their self-published books, which they use in their classes, are also available to the public. *Out of Your Mind — and into the Marketplace* gives step-by-step procedures to start a business. There are several books in the series; they each cost $25. You can request them through your local library before you decide if you want to buy one or all.

12

TO INCORPORATE OR NOT TO INCORPORATE

Now that you've located and absorbed more information on business than you ever thought you'd require, you need to think about your type of organization. You may find that forming a corporation is your best bet. Or it may be wrong for your circumstances. If you make a poorly informed decision initially, you may suffer unnecessary tax liabilities. The point is: make sure you collect *all* the information you need — in advance.

Let's talk about ways to organize your business. Most of you will be the sole proprietor. That means you, and you alone, own and are responsible for all business conduct. Most of the businesses in this book are of that variety.

THE MOM-AND-POP BUSINESS

Some businesses seem to be partnerships, as in *mom-and-pop* businesses. The two share responsibilities, but still only one person's name, or the family name, is on the business license. The other person is legally considered an employee. The following tale is of two people who share in the performing of their business, but it is legally a sole proprietorship.

Custom Guttering
Dwight and Sharon Saunders

After 34 years as a mechanic for Armour Packing Company, Dwight Saunders thought he was set for a good pension. Three months short of the 35 years needed for that pension, he was out on the street. A friend of the Saunders in their Minnesota town had a gutter business and talked Dwight into trying it.

"I'd worked on side-jobs around houses and construction all my life, so I knew installing gutters was something I could do. Besides, I've always been a handy, fix-it kind of person so the work itself didn't scare me, but the book work and finding customers did."

The Saunders spent $6,000 on equipment, including the machine that forms the aluminum into gutters, and supplies, such as fifteen-foot ladders. They set up shop in the back of their pickup and headed for Dodge City, Kansas, where Sharon's family lived.

From the beginning this was a true *mom-and-pop* operation. Since the gutters are long and unwieldy but not heavy, Sharon is as adept on the ladders as Dwight, only balking at hanging off roofs to nail the gutters in place. She takes care of all the bookkeeping, too. Things were slow at first, but within the year the Saunders were known for performing a good job, charging a reasonable amount and always being on time.

"One time when we went out to do a house, it would have been about a $100 project, but soon a neighbor came over and asked for a bid, so I did that one. Then another person drove up and the same thing happened. We did $700 worth of business that day and that's kind of the way the business has gone. I'm not always sure when I wake up where I'll have been by nightfall."

Much of their business is guttering older homes when gutters are required for loan approval before the houses are sold. They also do commercial structures and new residential buildings. Dwight says, "I'll go wherever I can make a buck," and sometimes that's been into Texas and Oklahoma. Now the Saunders have hired a retired fellow so they can do an average house in about four hours. An average house costs about $400 at $4.50 a linear foot.

"I tell people if they're home they can pay me right then. Or else we'll come do it, if you're home fine, if you're not, check it out when we get done. If it suits you, mail me a check or else tell me what's wrong so I can come fix it." Only two customers in the six years have reneged on their bill.

Dwight feels the biggest headaches have been government rules and taxes.

"If I'd known then what I know now, I'd have been scared to death. There's sales tax, unemployment, Social Security, workman's comp, state tax. It seems every time we turn around, they're after me for something else."

For a time, the Saunders had the guttering contract for a Sears Home Improvement Center which assigned them plenty of work, but now most of their contacts are by word of mouth.

"I think my age has made it easier for me to talk with people," Dwight says. "But more than six hours a day on the ladders gets to be too much. That's why I like setting my own hours."

One house that stuck in his memory had a *big* dog in the backyard — loose. The Saunders hauled the gutters up over the roof so they didn't have to try to set the ladders by the dog.

"Once in a while I get snappy and Sharon just tells me to quit fussin' at her," Dwight laughed. "But mostly we get along real good. This business together has been a good thing."

LOTS OF EGGS IN THE BASKET

As you read, you'll find several examples of entrepreneurs combining two businesses under one name. For instance, Lee Roddy in Chapter 2, who both writes and speaks, or John Frank, Jr. in Chapter 9, who piggybacked one business onto another. While the Jameses take the prize for the most enterprises in one household, they are still a sole proprietorship.

Homestead Enterprises
Stanley and Vivian James

Grandma used to say, "Don't put all your eggs in one basket." Business-ese defines the principle as *diversification*. In this age of specialization, Stanley and Vivian are living, breathing examples of entrepreneurs who have combined several small businesses into one busy and growing enterprise.

They sold their 60 dairy cows and the farm to retire. At the time, they kept 35 acres on the back corner of the home place and 47 wooded acres close by. They also kept some of the machinery, notably a portable saw mill and tractors with mowers, brush hog and rotovator. The idea was to build their dream home and travel with their newly purchased motor home.

"I'd always dreamed of owning a bed and breakfast," Vivian said, "so when we built this house we put two bedrooms with baths at one end and our bed and bath at the other. The sliding glass door in front of the dining table looks out over the deck where the birds feed. We had five pairs of cardinals nesting in our yard last year. The coyotes and foxes trot through our yard, and in the fall, the turning leaves paint a different picture each day. Needless to say, guests are booking repeat visits."

Although she doesn't cook a full farm breakfast because so many people are concerned about cholesterol these days, there's a wide variety of toast, muffins, fruits, cereals and beverages set out on the counter. Since both the Jameses work away from home during the week, guests come just on weekends. Vivian says she and her husband have traveled the world through the eyes of their visitors from England, Australia and France.

That's one business.

When someone wants to turn his timber into lumber, he calls Stanley with his portable sawmill. The mill, attached to a trailer, travels behind the pickup and can be set up for jobs as short as an hour or for days at a time. James charges by the hour, $25 per, plus $25 for each blade used, all with a $50 minimum. He says that in the first two months of '90 he's done as much business with this outfit as in all of '89. He turns all kinds of trees into raw lumber, whatever dimension the owner desires. Stanley's current project is a set-up in a boat yard on Lake Champlain. There he is sawing white oak, including the knees (where branches join the trunk) into joints and other lumber for a schooner being built like those in our early history.

His other two rigs are equally portable. Instead of producing smooth boards, his tractor and six-foot brush hog knock down and grind up trees and brush up to about three inches in diameter.

"Actually anything the tractor bucket can knock down, the hog will grind up," James said. For this land-clearing operation he charges $35 an hour. The smaller garden tractor and rotovator are used for prepping local gardens. After he makes two passes with the tiller, the ground is ready to plant, with little raking needed. For this he charges $45 an hour. Any gardener who's ever bucked a hand rototiller knows the value of this service.

Those are businesses number two and three.

Number four is seasonal too. When the sap runs, the Jameses hustle full speed ahead as they tap their acres of maple trees, boil the sap down to syrup and seal the finished product into cans for sale. B&B guests frequently purchase cans of syrup for themselves or friends and orders come in from the surrounding vicinity. Syrup can be purchased in cans sized from one pint up to a gallon.

If all this weren't enough, Stanley and Vivian both hold outside jobs. She works full-time for an organic baby food company called Earth's Best and he works part-time picking up milk samples from local dairies for the Federal Milk Market Administration. Stan also dabbles in real estate, which is growing to be more productive.

They haven't had to advertise much, since word of mouth, the yellow pages, *The Gold Pages* and referrals from close-by Middlebury College, Vermont have been enough to keep them busy.

"I do all the bookkeeping and record keeping," Stanley said. "That's the only way a business owner knows what's happening in his business. All our endeavors seem to mesh so while we can be really busy at times, I still enjoy the feeling of being in control. I am my own boss and I love the things I

154

do. I give good service at a fair price, and although we'll never be millionaires, we can take time to play with our six grandchildren when they visit. Maybe one day we'll try traveling again. We sold the motor home with only 600 miles on it. But then again maybe we won't. We might just let the world beat its way to our front door. Folks couldn't find a better place to sit and rest a spell, and watch the seasons change."

INCORPORATION

"A corporation is, hands down, the best way to structure most businesses. . . it has that great, stupendous characteristic called limited liability. The people who own it are not liable, responsible or accountable for its actions," says Paul Hawken in *Growing a Business*.

The trick is deciding what kind of corporation to form, as there are several different types. You'd be wise to contact an attorney or SCORE for advice as to which would be most appropriate for your business. Most small businesses opt for the S corporation designation rather than the C corporation, which allows income or losses to flow through to you directly, giving you a tax advantage either way.

Alpha Services and Acme Accounting
Charles E. Landers

Charles Landers had the peculiar honor of teaching his oldest daughter in grade school, high school and finally in college. But his income from teaching was never enough to support a wife and three growing daughters, so he moonlighted in everything from selling cars to income tax preparation. The latter stuck.

When St. Mary's of the Plains College phased out his department that included nuclear physics, atomic physics and mechanics, Landers had a choice. He could move out of state to another college position or go into business for himself.

"I chose to go with accounting and tax preparation full-time," he said. "My daughters were in school and my wife taught home economics in the local high school so uprooting us all seemed unfair. My friends and clients all said, 'Stay in Dodge City and we'll help you find business,' so we did. I had a number of rentals at the time and with my wife working, I knew we wouldn't starve until I got this business off the ground."

He named his new S corporation *Gamma Lambda, Inc.* (formed to save taxes) with the principles being himself, his wife and a daughter. They now employ two secretaries because the business grew rapidly. Landers services 500 smaller accounts and six corporations that each do over $500,000 in business a year. Last year *Gamma Lambda, Inc.* grossed $60,000.

Lander's advice to new business owners comes from his own experience. "Start out in your home if you can, to keep the overhead down." He still runs his business out of his basement office, which now includes a full complement of computers and office machines.

"Work in an area of the business before you jump in for yourself." He moonlighted for years. "I see too many people go for their Ph.D. with the goal of teaching when they've never taught. I tell them to get their Bachelor's degree and try teaching a few years to see if they're any good or not.

"Start small. Part-time during the tax season can be called starting small.

"Keep good records. More people go broke on paper than in the business." Charles has always kept meticulous records. He suggests hiring a good accountant if you aren't trained yourself.

"Have a separate bank account for your business. You'll never believe the messes I've straightened out when people ran their personal and business accounts together."

Landers has never done any advertising; all his business has come through word of mouth. "That backs up my most important advice: give good service and stand behind your work. If people trust you, they will recommend your service to others."

Charles sees his age as an advantage in his business. "People look at my gray hairs and lines and think, 'He must know his business. He's been around awhile.' I have and I do."

FOR ADDITIONAL INFORMATION

Remember that you choose the structure of your

business both for legal reasons and to save yourself taxes and headaches. Bob and Jean Lamb in Chapter 11 incorporated, as did Rick Frederick in Chapter 14. Al Edwards, however, went into his head-hunter business with a partner, forming a partnership (see Chapter 1).

While you are planning your new business, find a good attorney — that's good advice.

GOOD READING

There's a good article, "Think Before You Inc.," in the March/April 1990 issue of *Entrepreneurial Woman*. Find it at your library, or write to 2392 Morse Ave., Irvine, CA, 92714.

13

PLANNERS RARELY FAIL BUT FAILURES NEVER PLAN

THE BUSINESS PLAN

"There is only one reason to do a comprehensive business plan and that is to take it to the bank for money," said Ron Horner, owner of Horner and Associates, Inc., a Georgia-based business consulting company.

Some people will tell you there are other good reasons to do a business plan, but the operative word here is *comprehensive*. We'll discuss different reasons and styles later in this chapter.

If you absolutely have to borrow to start or operate your business, taking the extensive time to complete a business plan is imperative. *Anatomy of a Business Plan* by Pinson and Jinnett (Out of Your Mind and Into the Marketplace, 1988) leads you step by step through the process.

The packet of information from the SBA has a good outline in *How to Raise Money for a Small Business*, prepared by Dun & Bradstreet.

An even simpler outline has been compiled by

159

Linda Chandler of Chandler Associates, a business consulting firm in Benicia, California. She suggests people start with the simpler form because it is not so intimidating.

Business Plan Outline

I. Name of Firm
II. Owner, owner-to-be
III. Information on business
    A. Type of business, and product/service
    B. History
    C. Office/Plant
    D. Personnel
    E. Economic/Accounting
    F. Inventory, supplies, equipment
    G. Legal
    H. Future plans — planning for change!
IV. Market Analysis
    A. Customers (market)
    B. Environment
    C. Competition
    D. Competitive advantage/disadvantages (assessment)
    E. Projections — planning for change!
V. Marketing Strategy
    A. Promotion/Sales strategy
    B. Pricing strategy
    C. Distribution strategy
    D. Product/Service strategy
VI. Management
VII. Financial Data

This gives you an idea about what financiers are looking for when you bring them your business plan. You have the option of having a professional do this for you, but doing it yourself will give you a good handle on your business. Just make sure you turn out a professional looking document, typed with no errors, good grammar, punctuation and spelling. You would be wise to hire someone to prepare your final copy if you don't feel proficient enough yourself.

Marilyn Thurau went about doing a business plan a slightly different way.

Summitteers Radiant Heat, Inc.
Marilyn Thurau

"I will not fail! I refuse to fail!" These vows kept Marilyn Thurau on track for the first year of her entry into the construction industry with a product called Flexwatt Radiant Heating. As a first time business owner and a woman in a man's world, sometimes gritting her teeth and grinning anyway was the best approach to knotty problems.

Using $2,000 in start-up capital raised from her own resources, her son and her husband, Marilyn opened a home-based office in Oakland, California. Of the original amount, $1,300 was paid to a lawyer for drafting the incorporation papers.

Marilyn knew she had an excellent product with plenty of sales territory, the entire West Coast. Since California's energy laws rule out radiant heat in new residential construction, Thurau focused her attention on multi-family construction, light commercial construction and remodels.

"I combed construction news, local papers, asked everyone I could about construction sites. I went door to door, cold-calling on architects to convince them to try my product. Home shows yielded only a few leads, but I sent my brochure and a sample to each one. Then I followed up with a phone call and/or a visit within a week. I credit my beginning success to that kind of intensive follow-up.

"I was determined to dispel the horror stories circulating about overhead electrical heating. Much of my job is to educate the construction industry from the architects down to the installing electrician about the advantages of my product."

Thurau has kept her finger on the pulse of her customers by delivering the supplies herself, checking back to see if there are any problems and always being available to answer questions or troubleshoot. She feels that by close observation she has learned where the snags can happen and how to forestall trouble.

Marilyn belongs to a number of business organizations and has gained much of her expertise through workshops and meetings offered for the construction industry by these specialized organizations, such as Women in Construction and Women Construction Owners and Executives — USA. Now she receives her notices of future construction through the *Pipeline*, a Bay Area publication and network.

"I knew I should put together a business plan to begin with, but if I had waited to do that, I might never have started. However, a completed business plan is my suggestion to those thinking of a new business. I did take my own advice though, by attending a series of classes through the East Bay Small Business Center. By the end of the six weeks I had a business plan in hand and a better idea of not only where I was going but how I was going to get there. The instructor walked us step by step through the process. I also found the Alameda County Business Library to be a good resource."

Marilyn, like many others interviewed for this book, feels that her age is an advantage. By this time in life, a woman has more freedom, the children are grown and there is usually a nest egg to draw on financially. When Marilyn's business needed an infusion of capital, she was able to provide it without having to ask a banker.

Since Thurau operates her business out of her home, she found it wise to rent a box at Mail Boxes, Etc., for a business address and to use their fax and copy machines when she picks up her mail daily.

"I can copy and fax on their machines a tremendous amount for what it would cost me to own my own. And besides, using that address keeps my home private, since I just walk downstairs to my office at eight every morning. My commute is a cinch. And I like the boss of the company — me."

A BUSINESS MAP
The second-best reason for composing a business

plan is to help you know where you are going. That's why I call it a map instead of plan. Since this is for your personal information, the map needn't be nearly as detailed as the plan, but should include your assets, your distribution system, a profile of your customer, balance sheets and income forecasts. Fill out this simpler form at the beginning of each year.

Paul Hawken gives excellent information on business plans and financing in *Growing a Business*.

Business plan for financing, or business plan for map, both help you understand your business and plan for the future. Many businesses fail to plan adequately, either for day-to-day, or for tomorrow.

One business person I know sets aside two hours every week for planning. She goes to a restaurant, orders a pot of coffee and plans her week. This way she is not disturbed by the phone, the over-flowing pile of "to-dos," or customers. A monthly session like this would be an advantage over no planning. You can use a part of this time to check back against your over-all plan for the year. Are you on target? Where do you need to make adjustments? Don't forget, in addition to helping you obtain financing, *planning* is what business plans are for.

FOR ADDITIONAL INFORMATION

Other contributors to this book have good information on business plans for you. Check Chapter 4 for Dave Richard's advice, or Landers in Chapter 12.

14

NEITHER A BORROWER
NOR A LENDER BE

There may be as many ways to finance a business as there are businesses. And in many cases, as with the wide variety of types of businesses, you are limited only by your own creativity. All through the book you've read tales of creativity, but most of us don't consider raising money as being creative.

The amount of financing will vary for each business, depending on whether you buy or build, and of course, what size business you start with.

Most people think first of a bank loan or possibly the "cheap" money they've heard is available through the SBA. Your business plan is essential for both these avenues.

Many of the people in this book have said, *Do not borrow.* That's excellent advice, but they've had to raise capital some way. Keep in mind that finding the money through your own assets is also borrowing, even though it is from yourself. The advantage is that you have no one else looking over your shoulder.

FINANCING BY OWNER CONTRACT

Let's look at buying a business through the eyes of a man who joined an already successful firm, both as a real estate agent and as a business broker.

Vermont Business Brokers
Maurice Diette

As an officer in a large commercial bank, Maurice Diette held the yea or nay power over business loans. His point of view was always, "Will this person's venture make money for my bank?" His will-this-make-money point of view now slants from a different angle as he seeks to help clients either sell or buy businesses.

Maurice planned his exit from 28 years of banking by earning his real estate license two years earlier. He and his family discussed the realities of striking out on his own; paramount in the discussion was the reality of no income for a time.

"I'd seen many in the 50-plus bracket just hanging on for the pension. I didn't want to be in that state. I knew I needed new challenges, a change; I call it the entrepreneurial itch. So I resigned from the bank, grateful for all the friends and contacts I'd made through the years, and joined this business brokerage. I knew my greatest assets at that point were the many people in my life whom I could call on for advice, encouragement and referrals."

The lean time didn't last long because Diette capitalized on his strengths and hustled.

"There were days," he said, "when my feelings of

self worth were on the bottom, but the tremendous sense of accomplishment I felt when sales started to close really charged me up. I knew I was making it on *my* efforts, my abilities."

Maurice says that about 50 percent of his clients searching for a business are over 50. Many of them have either taken early retirement or been strongly encouraged to do so. They know they need to do something else and want to stay in the area. Diette also gets many people who want to leave the rat race of the cities; to them Vermont seems a bit of heaven.

The *Business Brokers* of Colchester, Vermont have a form they ask prospects to fill out, indicating desire, financial ability, needs, wants and probable time-line.

"If someone has been looking for a year or two, they probably won't make up their mind any time. If this is a spur-of-the-moment idea, lookers aren't too viable either. But if they've given several months of serious thought to the idea of a business, then I know they're likely candidates."

Likewise, on the other side, Maurice helps a business owner determine how much his business is really worth. The most difficult assessment is the value of good will, how loyal the customer base.

"Many times business owners show their faith in the business by agreeing to hold part of the contract. They also agree to train the new owner, usually for a week or two, but they can contract for longer on a consulting basis.

"When banks are tight with money, like right now, both buyers and sellers have to be more creative to make their transaction work." Diette said an average business with five or six employees runs between $250,000 and $300,000 in his area, with the gross dependent upon the type of business. Diette recommends that people do an in-depth self-analysis before they think of buying a business.

1. What is your financial picture? Assets, liabilities. For assets: do you own your home? How much equity? Do you have investments, life insurance, savings? A liability is anything you owe money on, any debts you have. When you total each and subtract the liability total from the asset total, you'll see your financial picture.
2. What kind of work do you like to do?
3. Are you customer- or number-oriented?
4. How's your family support? Is your spouse able to support the venture both emotionally and financially?
5. What skills can you bring from past experience?

Diette also has some suggestions. "You're better off if you can remain in a locality where you're well-known. Friends and acquaintances are a tremendous asset.

"You must search to find the place where you will fit into the marketing scheme of things. Don't try to do it all.

"Starting over after 50 isn't for everyone. But if you can endure the emotional roller coaster and persevere, the freedom from a boss looking over your shoulder is worth any effort."

SELLING ASSETS TO BUY A BUSINESS

We've seen buying a business from the point of view of the broker. Now let's jump to the other side of the fence and visit with some folks who went through a broker to find their first business.

Four Seasons Gift Shop
Will and Jonnie Boudry

Through a business broker, Will and Jonnie Boudry learned of a cigar stand for sale in the lobby of an office building in Thousand Oaks, California. What sold them was the fact that 1600 female employees weren't allowed to leave the premises for lunch or snacks. They sold their vacation cabin to pay for the business.

Within a year they had changed the type of inventory from cigars to things women want, built the 300-square-foot business large enough to move across the lobby to an additional 90-square-foot space, added coffee, doughnuts, soft drinks, a line of cards and gifts, and knew all their customers by name.

Will was no novice to the retail industry. He'd designed fixtures for large retailers such as K Mart, and well understood use of space and how to stock for premium sales. Jonnie knew how to give good service and listen to her customers' wants and needs.

Service, convenience, listen, be gracious: four keys to retail success parlayed this small start-up business in one tower to the addition of a second, larger site in the sister tower of the same office building. When the building manager offered Will 3,000 square feet of space, he and Jonnie leaped at the chance to open a full-service coffee and gift shop. Customers could select wrapped sandwiches, salads, fruit and yogurt from the self-service refrigerators, pour either hot or cold drinks at the drink bar and eat at the tables or in their offices.

On the aisle to the food, customers passed gondolas of cards, gifts, jewelry, cosmetics, candy, whatever little things that might catch their eye. Pet Rocks were a hit in their time, as were peanut plants in tiny containers. Jonnie was always on the lookout for the latest fad or gimmick that her customers might enjoy.

The Boudrys even ran their own credit line with a 3x5 card for each customer. No matter the size of the bill, the service charge was $2, due on payday.

"It's pretty hard to cheat someone who calls you by your first name," Will said. "We never had any trouble collecting accounts and this way, the women spend more freely. Our customers knew they could always find the last-minute gift or card or an emergency item with us."

The Boudrys had invited a daughter and son-in-law into the business at the opening of the second store with an investment of $30,000. At about the same time, they added a third store in another office building. In that location, customers had to walk through the gift store to get to the separate cafeteria, so while business did all right, it was never the money maker of the first two.

Each new site was purchased with money from the previous, so the Boudrys were never in debt, even though they were running a large inventory. "About $50,000 in the original *Four Seasons*," Will said.

"We loved going to the gift shows," Jonnie added. "We went to Las Vegas, Los Angeles, San Francisco, and those were vacation times, too. We loved doing our business and providing the kind of service that made life easier and lighter for the women in our building."

Fear crept in when the area around the Twin Towers deteriorated. Several merchants were killed in the neighborhood and another raped in the underground garage, so the Boudrys decided to look elsewhere for their dream, a true gift shop. They sold the shops at handsome profits, and sold the original *Four Seasons* back to the first owner. He was a Korean gentleman who never could figure out why he sold the space in the first place, since the Boudrys had done so well with it.

"We learned a lot in those years," Jonnie said. "Mostly about people. The amazing thing was, the poorer the woman, the more jewelry she would buy. The rich are harder to sell to.

"It is so important to build trust, especially in a closed situation like we had. We saw many of our customers every day. We knew who bought which brand of cigarettes, ate which candy bars and how the diets were going. We knew about their families, cheered for them in the good times and cried with them in the bad."

"We learned how hard it is to find good employees and even more difficult to keep good caterers," Will added. "You should have heard the furor the day a customer found a beetle in her wrapped sandwich. It was on to the next catering company for us. But all in all, we made money and had fun doing it."

"It was a shame we didn't stop there, after the sale," Jonnie said. "Because our high quality gift store in a wealthy area didn't do well at all. We should have taken our own advice, which was that the rich are harder to sell to, but then hindsight is wonderful. Again we learned a lot, but this time much of it was negative."

Will and Jonnie's advice is still: 1. Do something you like. 2. Do *not* borrow. 3. If you expand, build the new one on the old. 4. Listen to your own wisdom. You learned and earned it.

"Being in business together was good for us," Jonnie said. "Will and I complement each other's skills, and one thing for sure, we never had time to be bored or worry about our aches and pains. Being in business helps keep you young."

"If I could just get my hands on a little cigar store..." said Will.

BUILDING A BUSINESS USING FINANCING

The following two businesses needed large infusions of capital, both to begin and to continue operating. They found their money in different ways, which might trigger some ideas for you.

Diaries, Inc.
Awareness Communications
Rick Frederick

"A goal without a plan is a daydream," is one of Rick Frederick's favorite sayings about the many and varied aspects of his businesses. He's a man willing to take risks because he knows he has combated one of the tougher addictions, alcohol, and is winning on a daily basis.

"When you have to ask for help and finally realize the strength you have within yourself is multiplied by the strength of your support group, you understand that life is all about caring for each other."

Rick speaks to corporations around the country on the cost of alcoholism in the workplace and how to recognize the problem. His book on this subject, *America's Billion Dollar Binge*, will be finished in the next year.

Rick left a PR position in the academic field to purchase and expand a travel agency. He took an active part in the community: chamber of commerce, service clubs, community events; all to promote his growing business. Travel agency owners travel to better help their customers, and it was during such a trip that another brainchild was born.

"'How do you keep track of all your pictures and memories?' was my question," Rick said. "I was looking through a hodgepodge of stuff I'd collected on one trip, not finding the item I wanted, of course, and wished for a diary to help me out. I went out to buy one only to discover there was no such product available."

The foreword of the first diary says, "The Traveler's Diary is designed to help travelers remember their experiences with an easy-to-use recording system which matches their photos and written information." In addition, there are sections on how to improve your photos, a complete list of travel tips and a comprehensive travel check list, combined with U.S. and International Tourism offices and addresses. Travelers need only a few minutes a day of travel time to fill in the blanks and so have information and memories recorded forever.

Always one to milk an idea dry, Rick thought of others who could use a similar diary: hunters, people who fish, birdwatchers, gardeners, the list continued to grow. Each book included information important to that particular activity and room for the private observations of the devotee. Frederick capitalized on well-known people in each field by incorporating their expertise in the diary and name on the cover, for example, *Uncle Homer Circle's Fishing Diary.*

Rick's ideas quickly outstripped his financial abilities. He sold the travel agencies to invest in publishing the diaries himself, then approached banks and other lenders for more capital. As a writer and marketer, he understood the importance of a well-thought-out business plan. Banks don't loan money on just dreams and good ideas. He also thought of selling interest in his company through venture capital.

"But I wasn't sure how much of the company I wanted to part with," he said. "I've never claimed to be a money person, but with the right infusion of capital, we could take the 23 different diary ideas I've copyrighted to a multi-million dollar company.

"I did some real soul searching at that time," Rick said. Lands' End, a clothing and luggage store and catalogue company, ordered 30,000 copies of the travel diary. Other orders came in. But the question persisted: did he want to devote *all* his time and energy to this enterprise? Or did he want to. . .

Travel, writing and corporate speaking won out. He and his wife bought a 40-foot sailboat, located a distributor for the diaries (Fredericks will be paid on a royalty basis), sold their home and possessions, and switched their mailing address to Kenosha, Wisconsin. They plan to spend at least the next year sailing the Eastern Seaboard, the Bahamas and the Great Lakes. He'll finish the book during this time.

"Planning is the key," Rick stressed. "I'm in the enviable position of not having to worry about money, but starting years ago, I set that plan in motion and worked toward the goal."

Rick tells anyone and everyone that they have to believe in themselves and in their dream or product, if they're in business.

"I fully support Gary Comer's philosophy. He's the owner of the successful catalogue company called Lands' End. He says:

1. Come up with a good idea.
2. Find a niche.
3. Research the dickens out of it. See what's really there. Check out the competition. See whether your idea and that niche you found are going to meld.
4. You need a bit of luck and good timing.
5. *Persistence* is the key to all success. *Do not give up*. Dream your daydream, devise and write out a plan, then put all your energy into action for that plan and your daydream/goal will become your reality. *It will happen*!

"Oh, and don't forget to enjoy yourself and the people you meet along the way," Rick finished. "They're your greatest treasure."

Goodyear Tires
Jerry Ohman

When you ask for Jerry Ohman at the *Goodyear*

Tire dealership you better designate younger or older, because father and son work together, as does the elder Jerry's wife. Their business was three years old in July, 1990 and caters to the trucking industry.

The other Goodyear store in town deals only with passenger tires, so the Ohmans carry tires for heavy equipment, farm machinery and logging trucks, and also have a busy on-the-road service. The shop does tune-ups, brake jobs and auto and truck repairs, in addition to keeping a full stock of tires, with over $250,000 in inventory.

The Ohmans chose Bemidji, Minnesota because it was the only major city in the three-state area that didn't have a full service tire business. The shop is located at a truck stop on Highway 2, so they get truckers from all the Midwest and even Canada.

Jerry had been in the tire business for 25 years, starting out with another supplier and then joining the Goodyear ranks. He managed stores in various cities around Minnesota and the Dakotas, but a friend kept after him to open a store in Bemidji.

"I just don't have the money for such an undertaking," Jerry told him, "so forget it."

"Well, I've got the money," the trucker friend said. "Let's go to the bank and see what kind of a deal we can work out."

When the bank said they needed more backing, Jerry called another friend and asked if he'd like to join the deal. The man agreed after he saw the need in the area.

"It was a strange way to put the package together," Ohman said. "But sometimes you do what you have to do, if you want the business bad enough."

The only real competition for truck tires was the Wednesday night round-up when salesmen would come from Fargo, Brainard, Grand Forks, Duluth, anywhere to sell tires in Bemidji. But they couldn't provide the service needed.

Jerry invited his son to join him after he was sure the money and building were available. When they opened, young Jerry took over managing the shop, older Jerry was the buyer and PR man and Mom took care of all the daily bookkeeping, the banking and payroll. They advertised extensively in newspapers and the radio for a 100-mile radius, especially to the truckers, farmers and loggers.

"Since we'd borrowed 100 percent, we didn't have any time to sit around. We had to get rid of all those tire salesmen who came in on Wednesday. They offered all kinds of cut rates to try to drive us out of business, but it didn't work. Business has been so good, I couldn't go out and do sales calls like I thought I'd need to. It seems we're always a man short around here so I just didn't have time."

Ohman found good men on the unemployment rolls to work for him. He pays them better than the average around town, so with all the overtime, his crew remains loyal. When things got too busy, the Ohmans offered to hire another man, but the crew dug in and worked harder, rather than give up their overtime.

"Customers often ask me where I got such a good crew," Jerry said, "because my men are always polite and give good service. I say, 'Off the unemployment rolls,' but my men stay because we treat them like human beings."

Jerry's advice to new business owners is, "Make darn sure you have good help. I'm fortunate because I could never have done this without my son, Jerry. I had no idea how good he was, but he went through all the training seminars like a pro and understands the business better than men who've been in it for years. He knows the business will be his, in fact my stock in the corporation is deeded to him. Someday my wife and I would like to spend time at our cabin and I feel secure knowing that Jerry is running the store."

FOR ADDITIONAL INFORMATION

Although "don't borrow" was the suggestion most often heard from the people in this book, many of them used "creative financing." Some other good examples are Al Edwards in Chapter 1, John Frank, Jr. in Chapter 9, and the Cooks in Chapter 16.

GOOD READING

A good book on the subject of money is *Moneylove* by Jerry Gillis, Warner Books, 1979. He helps you discover where you learned your ideas about money, and how it should be spent, earned or saved.

15

NIFTY WAYS TO TELL JOHN Q. PUBLIC WHO YOU ARE AND WHAT YOU SELL

In this chapter we'll talk about the ins and outs of advertising, starting with direct mail.

DIRECT MAIL

Direct mail has come to have a dirty name in this country where mail boxes are loaded to the gills with hype of every type. In spite of its bad press, direct mail is a profitable way to advertise, or why would companies continue to do so?

The knack in making it work for you is to first understand the system and then apply it to your own business. Basically, the purpose is to get your information into the hands and minds of your would-be customers in the speediest and most economical way possible. You can choose to go for the big numbers by sending out hundreds of thousands of pieces, as does the Publisher's Clearing House Sweep-stakes or you can reach your market in myriad smaller ways.

For instance, the local cleaners has a coupon in a booklet mailed according to zip codes to the people in its immediate area.

Ron Horner & Associates, Inc.
Ron Horner

"Remember that your goal with direct mail, as with any advertising, is to sell your product. Most people give up too soon. Statistics show that most sales are made between the fifth and eighth contact. Most salespeople give up after three 'no's.' I've put together a direct mail program for small business owners," Ron Horner said, "who can't afford the gigantic mailing lists but need to expand their customer base."

Horner retired from corporate life, knowing that he would build a business of his own, possibly as a public speaker and/or trainer. He found that "Speakers and trainers are the worst self marketers around, second only to doctors, lawyers, CPAs and blacksmiths." There was a veritable gold mine to be found in marketing to such professionals.

Ron had, he admitted, "turned my head and stuck up my nose when computers were mentioned," but he finally gave in and the rutted road to that gold mine turned into a paved highway. He designed a program to market to speakers and writers, and discovered it would work for any small business. Now when Horner takes on a client, he provides the service he describes below, right up to the phone call.

"The first step is to figure out who your customer is," Ron said. "Where, when, why and what is she buying? How much money does she have? Does she *need* your gizmo or must you first create a desire? Where does she live, who are her neighbors and what do they buy? This kind of information is provided by companies who specialize in demographics.

"Once you know who your customer is, then you must decide how to sell to her. One method is by purchasing a specialized list from a local mailing list broker. You'll be amazed at how specific those lists can be. Your next choice is whether to buy or rent the list. You'll be wiser to buy the list, so that you can use it more than once. Since you plan on a full mailing campaign, you must have unlimited usage. If you rent the list, you purchased permission to use it only once. Some people think they can rent a list and re-use it, but list brokers have safeguards built into their lists, so they can catch cheaters."

The next step Ron recommended is to draft a series of three letters that will be sent within one week of each other. While the computer can put these out, there are some cardinal rules to follow.

1. Do not use address labels. Most people throw direct mail (junk mail) away and labels scream "mass mailing!" With a laser printer, an address looks like it has been typed right on the envelope; otherwise hand-address or type each piece.

2. Follow up with a phone call as your fourth con-

tact. Only mail as many letters at a time as you can follow up, even if that is only ten pieces a day. The purpose of your phone call is to get your prospective customer in the door to at least look. Remember, buying may not come until later.

3. Follow up those who seem at all warm on the phone call. Your next contact can be another mailing, a special sale, an invitation to an event, something to keep your name in front of the prospect. Then plan on a mailing or personal contact once a quarter. Contact like this is a sound plan for your regular customers too. Show them that you appreciate their business.

"A one percent return is average on mass mailings, but you improve your statistics when you follow these rules," Ron said. "Follow-up is the key. Being persistent and consistent with your direct mail, as in all areas of your business, helps change the numbers in your favor.

"You can do the steps yourself or you can hire them done. Either way, remember that a sales letter is a special kind of writing. That letter is your first impression on your customer, so make sure it is a positive one. No typos, grammatical errors, poor sentence construction, misspelled words. Be certain the person's name is spelled correctly, but you must depend on the quality of your mailing list for that information.

"When you learn to use the proper system, direct mail can be profitable," Horner said. "Just remember the most important point. Persistence pays."

NEWSPAPER ADVERTISING

The first place most people think of advertising is the local newspaper. In fact, most of your advertising dollars will probably be spent in newspaper advertising. You have a choice between display ads, those you see scattered throughout the paper, and classified ads, the two- or three-liners in the last section of the publication.

A display ad can be developed in several different ways: you can design it yourself, hire an advertising firm to design your ad or work with the graphic art department of the paper to create an ad especially for your business. Both good and bad ads come out of each approach, so remember one thing: a good ad is one that catches the reader's attention and gets him to contact your business.

Look through the paper and see what ads catch your eye. Study them. Do they tell the reader what special benefit the product or service will be to them? Do they have plenty of white space? An easily understood message? Good art work? Do they include phone number and address, including zip? What colors do they use, if any? What do you like about that ad?

Many newspapers offer seminars on advertising for their clients. Attend them; they're usually free and very informative.

After you have produced your ad, repetition is important. Smaller ads run on a regular basis are usually more effective than large, splashy ads run infrequently.

Rutland Playhouse, Inc.
Patricia Pratico

Teaching drama to high schoolers in the Phillipines took up 35 years of Patricia Pratico's life but, although she retired from the classroom, she couldn't retire from children or the theater. When she moved to Vermont she joined a local theater group and put on performances in schools, churches, or whatever building had room for an audience. Her favorite performers were children putting on plays for other children.

"When 2,400 square feet of space became available in a commercial condo, I bought it," Patricia said. "That sounds simple, but it wasn't. At age 68 I've learned more than I ever thought I wanted to know about legal and business terms.

"Just remodeling the space was a major undertaking. I'd been a school teacher all my life, not a business woman. But my 140-seat theater opened in September of 1989, and is well appreciated as the only stage in the area for live performances. Besides plays, we've shown foreign films and hosted touring groups for the community."

Display ads in the local newspaper, press releases and posters and fliers distributed in the area are excellent forms of advertising for these dramas or community events.

Rutland, Vermont is both fortunate and culturally richer since Patricia decided to settle there. She says she's the fortunate one.

"I guess I proved that you're never too old to learn, and have a great time doing so."

OTHER PUBLICATIONS

Don't depend only on newspapers for your print advertising. Check out local magazines and publications especially those designed to promote your type of business. Again, the library is a good source, as are the yellow pages.

Bed and breakfast businesses are ideal examples of using a variety of publications for advertising.

Packard House Bed & Breadfast
Vincent and Elizabeth Messler

Packard House, a 1790 Georgian-style home, reigns in the heart of Bath, Maine, the city of ships. The Messlers purchased the house from one of the Packards, a family once known world-wide for their ships.

The Messlers restored the house to its former glory and thus began their dream of owning a B&B in an antique house in an antique town.

Elizabeth loves to cook, so full breakfasts are a staple at *Packard House*. A meal might be a soufflé, special French toast, blueberry pancakes, home-made rolls or muffins.

Knowing the importance of good advertising, the Messlers helped form the Bath Area Bed and Breakfast Association and designed a group-advertising program for local and area publications. They joined the Bath Chamber of Commerce immediately and credit that organization with much of their success. The Maine Publicity Bureau has also been beneficial for them.

"You have to be active in your community," Vince said. "It's not just good business practice, but adds to your enjoyment of both life and your business."

Apple Valley Bed and Breakfast
Jayne and Bill Lilieholm

Apple Valley B&B guests look out their bedroom window to Lake Champlain and the Green or Adirondak Mountains. They have spent the night in a Federal house, listed in the state historical ledgers and belonging to the Lilieholms.

"I'd always dreamed of a home like this," Jayne said. "But my family kind of pushed into opening up a B&B."

She says she's never been sorry, even though getting a license and a tax number took some time. Since they only have two rooms to rent, unless they give up their bedroom, they had no trouble with the health department, either.

Jayne serves a full breakfast with blueberry pancakes and Vermont maple syrup as the house speciality.

Jayne joined the Shoreham Chamber of Commerce, which she says is still their best referral system, that and word of mouth. They listed *Apple Valley B&B* in the yellow pages and also *The Gold Pages,* a directory of local, home-based businesses.

"You can't really expect a business this size to support you," Jayne said, "but, since we're retired, it adds to our income. We meet people from all over and it isn't long before strangers become friends."

DESIGN YOUR OWN PUBLICATION

Trumpet Exchange
Richard J. Dundas

The *Trumpet Exchange* is a perfect example of niche marketing. Music stores and wholesale houses sell most of the new, and some used, musical instruments in this country. They often contract with band teachers to provide instruments for students, especially beginning players.

Richard Dundas had played trumpet in high school and college and now, 30+ years later, after a career in the university hierarchy all the way to president, he's back to playing around with his horn. And providing brass instruments for others around the country — at reasonable prices.

"I spent a lot of time in New York researching when I looked for a horn for myself. I tested trumpets never heard of in Rutland, Vermont. I wanted a good, modern instrument, but not at new prices."

Richard started collecting used trumpets to study

and resell in his area and soon began getting requests from all over the state.

"I placed a small inexpensive ad in a 16,000-member quarterly brass association newsletter. The response was amazing. Each issue brought letters and phone calls with offers to buy, sell or trade trumpets."

He visited trade shows and contacted manufacturers to expand his knowledge so he could buy and sell intelligently. He now has about 30 instruments on hand and traveling around the country, as he ships the horns via UPS for buyers to try out.

In 1986 he compiled all the information he'd collected and published 1,000 copies of a book titled, *Twentieth Century Brass Musical Instruments in the United States*. There is now a revised version and a German translation coming out of this authoritative study on modern brass instruments.

Richard uses the book to promote horn sales and vice versa. He also produces a list of available instruments which he sends to those on his mailing list.

"I add to my inventory by frequenting pawn shops, flea markets, garage sales, music stores, and of course, from other dealers and collectors," Richard said. He has an agreement with an antiue dealer: if he finds an instrument anywhere, Richard will pay him double what he paid for it.

Dundas is the first to say this kind of business isn't profitable enough for a full-time profession. But it provides him with outside contacts who like the same thing he does. And there's always something to do: repair a horn, mail letters, take a trip and look for horns and answer requests. As a bonus, the business brings in cash to supplement his pension.

"Letting enough people know what you do is a key to success," he advises business starters. "Don't think of just ads in the local papers. Use every avenue available to you, such as newsletters and magazines in your field of interest. Get yourself written up in any newspapers you can. My book is continually producing contacts.

"And always expand the network of people you know. Word of mouth is always the most effective form of advertising for any business started by a person of any age. And it only costs you what you want to give anyway — a good product at a reasonable price with the kind of service you wish businesses would give you."

PROMOTIONAL ITEMS

Ad-Craft
Neil Vold

Neil Vold didn't just retire *from* the Farmer's Union Central, a local gasoline co-op, he retired *to* a business he'd already planned and put into place. Since he'd traveled around the Dakota area for the gas company for years, he knew every business and farm owner for hundreds of miles. He also knew how important advertising is, especially promotional items.

190

Neil had lined up a supply house called *Ad-Craft*, so when he signed up with them as a sales distributor, he became an independent agent operating his own business but using the company as his source. Armed with company catalogues and a variety of sample pens, key chains, rulers, cards and calendars, he began his circuit. He called on those he knew and asked for referrals to the few he didn't. When he didn't make a sale the first time, he went back again.

"I thought this would be an interesting business," he said, "and an easy one to start since I already knew everyone. I liked the travel, I was used to it, but now I could set my own days and hours."

Vold operates his business out of his home basement office in Grand Forks, North Dakota and, of course, the trunk of his car. Orders are shipped directly to the customer with individual messages, addresses and phone numbers imprinted on the article in colors of the customer's choice.

"Sometimes I sell jackets or hats," he said, "maybe for a ball team or for a company to give their employees. Mostly I sell small items, ordered by the hundreds or thousands. Banks are good customers, especially before fair time when they order their give-aways."

Vold knows he could build his business larger, but he left the gas company to get away from the pressure. Why add more now?

"This keeps me busy enough," he said. "I can't be

like some of the retired people I know who just sit and do nothing. I'd be climbing the walls."

So his advice is to plan for your retirement. Realize that you'll feel better and be healthier with productive activities to look forward to. And if they make money for you, so much the better. Everyone can use a little extra once in a while — or all the time.

CARDS AND FLIERS

Mary Kay
Babs Hicks

When Babs Hicks had to retire from nursing because of her high blood pressure, she thought the world had come to an end. She was afraid she would no longer be useful.

When a friend encouraged her to have a facial to help her get over the depression, Babs found a business of her own.

Although the original investment seemed huge at the time, she now carries about $10,000 in inventory and has remodeled a room in her house in Yuma, Arizona into an office and display area for her 400 customers. Part of Bab's bookkeeping system is a card for each of her customers. This card lists name, address, phone, birthday, products used and date of purchase.

Babs says that one thing she does that works is budget a large amount of money for birthday cards and stamps. Each of her customers receives a birthday card every year, mailings with specials on products and the publicity the company provides. Hicks credits much of her repeat business to her mailings, the cards especially. This way each customer knows she is appreciated. While Hicks has tried other forms of advertising, the cards and word of mouth are what she believes helped bring her gross to $14,000 in 1989.

NEWSLETTERS

Another excellent advertising tool that can be used by most businesses is the newsletter, a project you can do in various ways. Some companies do in-house letters that go to their staff to keep them up-to-date. Others produce a letter to be mailed to their customers. This could include product information, news of sales, special promotions, and articles of interest in that line of enterprise. This letter could also be mailed to potential customers, using a purchased mailing list or via zip-coded mailing.

The Hortons in Chapter 16 devised a newsletter that goes to their *Gold Pages* group membership.

Whatever you decide, make sure the finished product looks professional. As with the direct mail program, the finished product must not only tell your message but it must *look good*. If done right, the results make the effort extremely worthwhile. If you want to pursue this idea but haven't the skills or time to produce the letter yourself, check your local yellow pages under editorial services, graphic designers and word processing services.

MONITOR YOUR ADVERTISING

Advertising has become a mega-buck business in this country. Every second we are bombarded by visual, audio and sensual messages. The three top reasons people buy a product are sex appeal, to save time and/or to save money. Watch the ads you see and hear to become aware of the three principles. You'll be amazed at how clever advertisers use your imagination to get you to buy their product.

A final note: monitor your advertising. Devise a simple sheet that lists the places you advertise. An example might be:

1 2 3 4 5 6 7 8 9 10

The *Sun*
The *Chronicle*
Yellow Pages
Building sign
Word-of-mouth
Mailing
Other

Then ask every customer, "How did you hear about us?" Tell them you are monitoring your advertising dollars so you know what's helping you the most. People will nearly always be gracious in their response. Put a hash mark in the appropriate box and at the end of the month or week, tally it up. Keep this form right beside the phone or cash register, depending upon where you greet your customers.

Advertising dollars are too important and too expensive to throw around, so take the time to monitor yours. If you've been in business for awhile and always give good service, I'd lay money that most of your responses will fall in the word-of-mouth column.

ANOTHER TIP

A good habit to develop: always send a thank-you note to people who assist you in any way. Include your business card. This takes time, but in the long run, you'll find it time well spent because of the quality of service you'll always receive. Thank-you notes really fall under the title of public relations, but there's a fine line between advertising and PR.

GOOD READING

Guerrilla Marketing by Jay Conrad Levinson, Houghton Mifflin, 1984. Gives excellent ideas for marketing that a small business with a limited budget can use immediately. One to read and reread — and use.

Words that Sell by Richard Bayan, Contemporary Books, 1984. A thesaurus to help you promote your products, services and ideas. Using this book will help you with fliers, letters, slogans, ads and other PR tools.

16

CREATIVE WAYS TO GET YOU AND YOUR BUSINESS IN THE PUBLIC EYE AND EAR

Webster defines public relations (or PR) as: "relations with the general public through publicity; those functions of a corporation, organization, branch of military, etc. concerned with informing the public of its activities, policies, etc. and attempting to create a favorable impression." In a word, sell, but in this case, more an idea or image than a product.

You can promote this image by the written word: for example, newspaper articles and press releases, advertising, newsletters, magazine articles, public service announcements, brochures and business cards.

Or use the spoken word: talk shows, public service announcements, business briefs, and advertisements on both radio and television. You can develop your skills as a speaker or teacher and shine in the public eye this way.

Stunts, activities and promotions using any and all

of these approaches and giving away either a service, a product or entertainment to your prospective customers is another method. Promote a local event; donate time or your name to a charity. The list goes on and on. Public relations for your company will be as wide and as effective as your creativity — or as those you hire.

Cronin Associates
Neil R. Cronin

"Free publicity? You did say free publicity?" Not an unusual reaction from his audience when Neil Cronin presents his *Ten Ways to Promote your Business without Spending Money* seminar to business people across the country and even in France and China.

"The first is press releases," Neil says, "Use any event in your company, like someone appointed to a new position, new acquisitions, honors given or received, a new or redone theory and application, anything that might be the least bit newsworthy. Write it up and send the typewritten copy to your local paper. You'll always find submission guidelines and a contact person listed in the paper on the day they run such business briefs. Keep your name in front of the public."

His second suggestion is to join associations and get on local boards, such as the water district, local Red Cross, or any service agency. You'll meet other business people and sometimes your name will be listed in the organization's press releases. Anything you can do to expand your network will be beneficial at some point in time. You'll also be known as civic-minded and a concerned citizen, good PR for your business.

His third suggestion is talk shows — television. This market is expanding and always needs new material. Figure out your hook, something that will grab an audience's attention. Cronin used all these techniques as he began his own training business in East Dennis, Maine after leaving a position as an academic dean and moving to Cape Cod. While he'd thought he was prepared for the change in lifestyle, both monetarily and in location, he still found himself suffering from culture shock. It sounds easy to chose a simpler lifestyle, but the doing of same is more difficult.

"But you persevere," Neil said, "and it begins to work. I found a need here for college classes, so worked with a college to bring the teachers to the Cape. We have a high percentage of retired folk here who really appreciate the chance to get a degree, even though the choices aren't that diverse."

Because he is fluent in several languages, Cronin discovered his niche in corporate training, both in the U.S. and France. His original topics in France explained American business practices to French executives.

"That's a one-shot thing, half a day to three days," Neil said. "I find that I'm not good with people one-on-one, but put me in front of a group and I love it. Besides, with this kind of training, I'm in and out. I resolved to never again take home briefcases full of work (my symbol of servitude) and I don't."

The business has now grown to the point where he is able to provide several other trainers with contracts, using a 70/30 fee division.

"If I can keep four trainers busy, it's more than one other me in financial returns."

Since the dollar is still low world-wide and the economy slow in New England, Neil is doing consistent business in France. Besides the corporate training, he is looking at ways to help American leaders of mid-size companies research the future markets in Europe. An immediate need is for locations where a business person can get travel and lodging advice, office help and space — literally a place to do business without setting up a full office. Another new venture is language tapes for Chinese businessmen and companies.

"When you lecture in China, you think your audience understands you," Neil said, "but in reality, they don't. These tapes teach business terms and systems.

"I think you must be more versatile if you want to get away from the big city and yet build a business that provides what you need, both in money and creativity," Cronin stated.

He has proven his versatility with his expansion into markets as they appeared, or as he saw a need and created a solution for that need.

"You *must* keep the overhead down," Neil repeated more than once. "If you try, you'll find creative ways to do that. Share an office, share secretarial help, work solely out of your home.

"Look at the customers you have: the maxim is 'there's gold in the old.' What other services or products do *they* need that you can provide? You have to spend some of your time developing new business no matter how busy you are servicing the existing accounts.

"Avoid things you don't like or don't do well," Cronin advises the over-50 business person. "By this time in life we have a pretty good idea where our strengths and weaknesses lie, so capitalize on that. Sometimes just chatting with someone else, maybe a career counselor, will help a person identify these areas.

"Make two lists, one for *what you do well* and the other *don't do well*. Then make sure the business you create utilizes your *do well* list. Let someone else do the other stuff. After all, we *are* getting older and age has its privileges — like being choosy."

PRESS RELEASES

A book I heartily recommend for anyone doing his own PR is *Handbook of Public Relations Writing*, by Thomas Bivins, (NTC Business Books, 1988). He gives excellent examples of different forms of PR work, advertising and even writing speeches. I've used his section on press releases in several of my seminars.

Briefly (and that's what most press releases are, brief), a press release is typed on your letterhead and mailed to a publication of your choice, usually the local newspaper.

YOUR LETTERHEAD

Contact person:
Phone day: night:
Release date and time:

TITLE GOES HERE, ALL UPPER CASE AND UNDERLINED, LIKE THIS.

The body of the release goes here. Double space, leave inch and a half margins, clean typing, and indent your paragraphs.

Use newspaper-style writing: the lead sentence should include who, where, what, why and how. Write your release with the most important information in the beginning and the following paragraphs in order of descending importance.

Check your local newspaper to see what style they prefer and to whom you send your release, plus the date it needs to be in to be published when you wish. Include a captioned black and white glossy photo if you desire, but don't plan on getting it back. Some papers are more amenable than others to publishing local press releases, but don't give up. Keep sending them out.

Press releases can have scope beyond your immediate area. These might be written with a bit different format. The opening should be a hook or grabber, with the factual information included later. This format could be used for distant newspapers, newsletters or trade magazines.

CREATIVE PR TOOLS

The following two businesses took a PR tool and built an entire business around providing that tool for others, at a profit for themselves.

Sound Word Associates
Richard and Doris Cook

Find a niche and fill it might be the byword for the Cooks as they provide taping, both video and audio, of conferences, seminars and classes. With their speed-duplicating equipment, the Cooks can sell the tapes right at the event for the attendees to take home. The Cooks give a copy of the masters back to the conference director or keep the tapes on file in their basement, which has nearly been outgrown by a booming business.

"You find those things that you can do well and that others can't or won't do and you build on it," Richard advised. Their services make other businesses more effective, more enduring, more available since the taping business includes mail order fliers and catalogues of their tapes.

Richard had been in the audio and video engineering and marketing field for 25 years before striking out on his own. He was able to purchase much of his original equipment from his boss at cost, so his initial investment was under $30,000, most of which he borrowed. The short-term loan was paid off quickly and he says that after that they've never been in debt more than $20,000.

"I think going into a business knowing this is your sole support is effective," Cook said.

"Sure, desperation makes you work real hard," Doris added. "Especially when you have children still in college."

The Cooks use their van to transport their equipment around the country but most of their business is within a five- to seven-hour radius of Michigan City, Indiana. If they need to fly, they usually don't tape entire conferences, but rather special programs.

Much of their business now is repeat so the Cooks have never done any advertising. It all comes by word of mouth from clients like Francis Schaeffer and his daughter Susan McCauley, who conduct a program called the Le Brie Fellowship, and from other yearly religious and educational conferences. Their best year yet was 1989 with a gross of $120,000, and 1990 already has twice as many engagements booked.

Realizing that someday they *might* want to cut back, the Cooks have invited their daughter and her husband to join them in the business. This now makes it possible for them to book simultaneous tapings.

"We don't plan to build an empire of this business," Richard explained. "We just do what comes along and keep our eyes and ears open for God-sent opportunities. For instance, one time we'd had an invitation and I had my doubts right from the first. But I had put this business in the Lord's hands with the agreement that I'd never turn down a call. We went — and I was right. We only sold about $100 worth of tapes.

"From the beginning our premise has been that our service would never cost the sponsor money for us to come. We pay our own travel expenses, donate ten percent of our earnings back to the program or performer and make our money by selling tapes. But $100 that night didn't even begin to cover our costs.

"However, that one was profitable in the long run because the speaker became very well-known and we had copies of his early tapes, including videos, all of which sell more and more. We have fliers and catalogues just for that group now."

Since people now use tapes and videos more as learning and teaching tools, the Cooks' recording business continues to expand.

They advise those who are thinking of a business to find their niche.

"Do your research so you know if what you want to do is needed. A good question is what segment of this industry isn't being met or not being done well? Can you do it better? Then do so.

"Don't begin with one foot in the protective pension plan. Don't just figure how much more you'll need to make to give yourself the salary you *need*. Go for the best your business can offer. The rewards are tremendous. And you have no idea of the wonderful people you'll meet. That makes every effort worthwhile."

Home Business Directory —
The Gold Pages
Pete and Bette Horton

Pete and Bette Horton not only run several small businesses of their own, one of them supports and promotes other home-based businesses in the central Vermont area.

"I knew we'd all be stronger if we stuck together," Pete said. "That's where the idea of the *Gold Pages* originated and the accompanying business group support and education program began."

The Hortons have a diverse background, from running a ski lodge to organizing a chamber of commerce to truck farming to tree farming. They believe in the necessity of small business to keep the economy going. They also believe in the strength of group effort, and once organized a marketing co-op for local truck farmers.

Their current ventures include writing columns and articles for local and regional presses, a Christmas tree farm (a long-term investment of time and labor), a small truck farm to sell produce locally,

The Gold Pages, a mail-order service for business books, speaking and bringing speakers to their support group for home-based businesses — and perhaps more by the time this book goes to print.

"When times get lean," Bette said, "we write another column — mine are on day-tripping — or an article. That seems to be our reserve income because we get paid promptly."

"We found a lack of respect for small, home-based businesses," Pete said, "and the desire to counteract that inspired *The Gold Pages*. After ghosting a book on corporate take-overs, we realized we'd rather write about the people around us, in their own businesses, whether they were farmers, writers, or inn keepers, working their own bits of real estate as they run their enterprises out of their homes. We thought maybe we should be networking with these people. So we invited those we knew of to a get-together here in Bridgeport, Vermont.

"From past experience we knew that any group needed a newsletter and a membership list so those members could contact each other. If we did a list, it needed to be a nice list, so we came up with *The Gold Pages*, meaning "opportunity," and set a fee for a business to be listed. This year it was $56 for the minimum listing and $92 for the larger, which includes art work. With this they receive four newsletters and can attend four meetings yearly.

"We have special racks where we distribute their literature along with the directory, and we help promote their businesses at whatever trade shows, home shows, seminars or anything we attend. We give away the directories at the Home and Garden Show and the country fair and in about a hundred other locations: supermarkets, banks, restaurants, wherever people congregate. We just ordered 8,000 from the printers, at a cost of about 75¢ apiece."

The Hortons are trying to build long term word-of-mouth for their advertisers, many of whom are hesitant to blow their own horns.

"Selling the concept to these people is the hardest selling job I've ever done," Pete said. "But we're beginning to see the results. We've learned that we must visibly support our 140 members by using their services and products whenever we can, and encouraging the other networkers to do the same."

The Hortons suggest that retirees have more assets to begin a business with than they realize. Maybe they haven't owned a business before, but many of the skills they used in their former jobs are transferable. With some additional education, through classes, books, tapes, personal advice and training, or finding a mentor, they can become the entrepreneurs they dreamed of being. Home-based businesses are becoming the "in" thing and older people are more adept at "living on the edge until the money comes in" than are their younger counterparts.

NETWORKING

"The term 'networking' was first popularized when it was named one of the ten trends of the 1980s in John Naisbitt's book *Megatrends* (Warner Books). In his book *You'll See It When You Believe It* (Morrow), Wayne D. Dyer says, '[Networking] means sending out into the system what we have and what we know, and having it returned to recirculate continually throughout the network. It means giving things away without any expectations." (From an article called "The Meet Market" by Susan Linn in Entrepreneurial Woman, March/April 1990.)

As the old saying goes, "It's not what you know but who you know." The following couple know a great deal about their craft, but they attribute part of their success to the countless people they have met through and for their business.

Norwegian Rosemaling
Lois and LeRoy Clauson

"The Norwegians decorate their homes and furniture with designs of stylized flowers, leaves and intricate brushwork done in oil paint," Lois Clauson explained. "This artwork is called rosemaling. Tole painting is similar but not nearly as complicated. Each district in Norway had its own refinements on the art and it is easy to determine where the artist lived by his painting."

Lois Clauson has become a master painter of rosemaling in this country, studying both in Seattle and Decorah, Iowa at the national Norwegian museum, and journeying to Norway to study the original works. She now teaches classes around Puget Sound and sells her own works at Pacific Northwest craft shows and exhibits.

As Lois's Bremerton, Washington business grew she was unable to find the high quality of wooden ware she needed for herself and her students, so when husband LeRoy retired, he entered the woodworking business. He has an excellent arrangement with his son Gary, who makes furniture as a hobby in his fully equipped shop. Dad uses the facility during the week, and son on the weekend.

Now LeRoy turns out Christmas ornaments, clocks, plates and formed wooden boxes called tina which the Norwegians use to carry meat or cheese. The shapes can be oval, round, or curved and are molded by soaking beech or balsa wood and forming it around a mold. He also makes a variety of shelves, and whatever project his customers desire. Besides producing wooden ware for Lois and her students, LeRoy sells his products wholesale to a local craft shop owner who has a catalogue service.

"I buy 1x12x2' clear (no knots) pine from Prineville, Oregon, birch from a lumber supply firm in Tacoma and a friend brought me a load of basswood from Minnesota," he said. "I can't compete with Taiwan for price but if someone wants a quality product, they know where to come."

One of the Clausons' best vacations was a trip to Iowa, where LeRoy spent a week learning how to make the wooden ware, and Lois studied brush and color technique, both at the National Norwegian Museum. Now some of their pieces are on display there.

The business has pretty much taken over their lives. They either prepare for a show, or sell at twelve different arts and crafts shows from May through July. They leave the business for the month of August and then begin preparing for the resumption of classes in September and more shows before Christmas.

Last year the business grossed around $14,000, "which doesn't begin to explain how much fun we had," they both agreed.

"Pricing the articles was hard at first," Lois said. "But the rule of thumb is six times the cost of the wooden ware. I hate painting Christmas ornaments but I can do one in about 15 minutes and they sell for $5, so that's the bread and butter of the business. Larger pieces take much more time and skill, but at least I've learned how to shorten the drying time. Most people use their cookie sheets for baking cookies in their ovens. Mine are for drying the rosemaling and you don't turn the oven on. Just crack the door so the light stays on. That's all the heat needed."

Lois said that they only needed a business license and a resale permit so they could buy at wholesale houses. Otherwise the cost of supplies, like oil paints, brushes and sand paper, would wipe out their profit. When she teaches, she hands out a supply list but usually carries a line of brushes so her students can begin with the quality that makes the brush strokes easier. And LeRoy supplies the wooden ware. Between the two of them, they help keep an antique art form alive — and growing.

The Clausons belong to several professional organizations such as Western Rosemalers, Sons of Norway and several museums. They credit their networking with much of their success both for retail and wholesale. Other than notices in the publications of these groups, they have done no advertising. They haven't needed to; if they had any more to do they'd need 30-hour days with eight-day weeks. It's a good thing they're retired, how else would they find the time to be so busy?

SOME TIPS FOR NETWORKING

Be a business card collector and giver. We all have trouble remembering names, but this way you have a tangible reminder of that last person you met. Then file those cards in a Rolodex. I usually write information about that person on the back of the card, especially any items I said I'd send on. On the front I write where I met the person and the date. Many times, the organization where I met my new contact triggers more information for me when I look back to find a service or contact in my file.

If someone you meet passes your name on to someone else and you receive business from the contact, make sure you drop a thank-you note in the mail right away. Treat your network associates with respect; they're one of your most valuable tools toward success.

Have fun with the people you meet. *How to Work a Room* by Susan Roane (Warner Books, 1988) gives wonderful suggestions to take the fear out of walking into a room full of people. The easiest method I know is to paste a smile on your face, stick out your hand and say, "Hi. My name is _____." A good follow-up question is "Tell me a bit about yourself, your business, what you like to do." Remember that other person is just as uncomfortable as you are and will appreciate your taking the initiative. Besides, you'll meet the most fascinating people this way. And, as so many of our experts have stressed, people is what business is all about.

COMMUNITY INVOLVMENT

Neil Cronin suggested community involvement as one of his ten steps for PR success. The following team is a good example of this principle.

Commercial Filter Service, Inc.
Bob and Ruth Wearley

Bob Wearley may not be flying commercial airplanes any longer, but he and his wife Ruth are flying high with their commercial air-filter company in Fort Wayne, Indiana.

Flying aircraft had been Bob's life, starting with the military, progressing to a long stint with Howard

Hughes, a few years with Singapore International, around the world to fly for Royal Jordanian Airlines and finally back in Indiana with Consolidated Airways. He always kept trying for the next level of expertise and when that ran out, he quit.

Happy to be back home but without a job, Bob began to look around for a business of his own, one where no one but himself could say how far he would go.

"Ruth and I work well together," he said. "We complement each other's skills, so we knew we wanted to work together for a change."

The Wearleys explored the idea of distributorships, flying to Texas to talk to an air-filter company. Disappointed with that company ("too promo-minded," Bob said) they met with a disenchanted distributor from the company who agreed to teach them the basics.

The Wearleys started their business on a shoestring. The station wagon they first used was a loaner. Through trial and error they researched until they found an air-filter (called media) that really did filter out the dirt. They construct the frames in-house so the tight fit increases the filter capabilities, filters which are mostly installed in commercial buildings.

Most importantly, they live up to their service contracts. *Commercial Filter Service* sells the product, constructs it and replaces the used filter on a pre-arranged time schedule, all for a lot less than their competitors.

The company is growing at a rapid rate, right on the projections that Bob had planned. They liquidated all their assets to start the business, but they still had borrowed "some pretty expensive" money from private investors. Four years later, they are in the process of planned debt-retirement.

Ruth is the company president and manages the office. Bob fills in wherever needed, selling, servicing, or hiring the growing number of employees.

"My whole philosophy," Bob said about getting good employees, "is to pay top dollar and get good people, train and motivate them, and then get out of their way." Bob said this was the best advice he could give to anyone starting a business.

Bob and Ruth believe in returning the good they've received to their community so are active in the Fort Wayne Chamber of Commerce and their church. Bob has recently been appointed to the Fort Wayne-Allen County Airport Authority.

"I have plenty of experience to bring to the board," Bob said, "from a pilot's point of view besides that of a manager, since I've flown into many airports around the world."

Bob used his flight years experiences in forming Aviation Explorer Post 2898 for boys interested in flying and aircraft. While he is no longer the leader, he serves as an advisor.

He is also on the board for a substance abuse treatment center and active politically so he doesn't have much time to waste. But that's the way with a person who cares not only about his business but about the community which he serves. Bob and his wife grow together, support each other, and have a good time along the way.

FOR ADDITIONAL INFORMATION

As you can tell from every person's story, word-of-mouth is the most effective form of advertising. Remember that each person will tell thirteen others of their bad experience, so it is your job to make sure all your customers have good experiences in dealing with you. Just think how many times you've tried a new product, a different restaurant, a new shop because someone *told* you about it.

You might reread this book looking specifically for the ideas on advertising and public relations. Almost every story has a tidbit to offer and you'll be amazed how many more ideas you'll generate for your own business if you jot them down.

GOOD READING

You Can Talk to (Almost) Anyone About (Almost) Anything by Elaine Cogan and Ben Padrow, Continuing Education Publications, Portland State University, Portland, OR, 1984. This book will help quell those butterflies and make it easier for you to speak in public.

KEEP YOUR EMPLOYEES HAPPY — THEY'LL STAY!

Our final business owner has some excellent advice on dealing with employees.

Holiday Inn, Fargo, N.D.
Wold Snack Foods
Clifford and Gladys Wold

Gladys has been Clifford's wife for 56 years, and he refers to her as his "right-hand man." The two ventured into the franchise business when he was 69 with the purchase of a Holiday Inn franchise in Fargo N.D. for $15,000. This was their idea of retirement from the optometry profession.

When Clifford first said he would build a hotel, there was considerable pressure to put it in downtown Fargo. However, he had a friend building a large business mall at the intersection of two state highways and that seemed the ideal location for a large convention-type hotel with spacious meeting rooms, lobbies and wide corridors for trade shows.

"I made three trips to Memphis, the headquarters for Holiday Inn, Inc., before I was able to get aptical — large lobbies cost, don't make money. After it was built, they sent many new prospects to look over our plant and plans. One reason for its success was the space for conventions. Now we've been given two awards by the Holiday system.

"One of those came in December of '88 at a group meeting of all 1600 inns. Our inn, one of the oldest in the system, was designated as one of the top 20. The award is based on many factors: few complaints by guests, general appearance and upkeep of property, profitability, etc. For the last three years, Memphis has never received a complaint from one of our guests.

"The success of any operation depends upon the people who work there, not just good management. Your people have to take pride in what they are doing, right down to the maid cleaning the rooms. If they don't have this feeling of pride, they're just pulling a paycheck. Many of our 320 employees began with us when they were attending school and pride has grown along with their knowledge of our business.

"We don't keep secrets. The more knowledge your employees have, the more they can make decisions and do a better job. We try to treat them as friends, more like family, and that helps create the pride we all feel."

All the decorating and quality control came under Gladys's umbrella. She chose the color schemes, wall and floor coverings, all furniture and fixtures.

Her interior design talent helped set the Fargo Holiday Inn apart from the others. But her high standards for housekeeping, food quality, service and general appearance of the place and the staff set the facility not only apart, but far above other Inns. Gladys's on-going encouragement assisted the entire staff in creating a welcoming atmosphere for the guests.

Because of her staff training, no guest has ever had a function fail in the Inn's history. That kind of record can make anyone proud and the Wolds make it a point to always make sure their staff hears about praise from customers.

Some long-time employees have been given shares in the company and many have been able to borrow money from the company to begin projects of their own.

Top management is shared between two of the Wold sons so the corporation is truly a family venture. Faith in their sons' abilities permitted Clifford and Gladys to again retire — this time to Scottsdale, Arizona where they lived through the winter months and headed home to Fargo each May or June. But even at age 80, Wold found time hanging heavy on his hands down there in the sun belt and began exploring other businesses.

A friend suggested a manufacturing company, turning raw nuts, sunflower seeds and popcorn into marketable snacks. After extensive research (the boys came down to check out Dad's new venture) they all knew the market was there — now to produce a product.

"The friend that encouraged me purchased used equipment, got cold feet and left," Cliff said. "I had invested about half a million at this point so I knew it was go ahead and learn the process from the bottom. I replaced the equipment with stainless steel to bring it up to top standards, hired a good sales manager who knew the area and the buyers, and took over the manufacturing.

"It wasn't long before we had an excellent product, called *Wold's Snack Foods*, and a good distribution system. I'm just grateful I had the capital to see us through until we arrived at the profit stage. It was a long, dark tunnel lighted with many prayers for help."

Two years ago the Wolds sold the company to a pair of Canadian brothers, making about a million dollars profit on the transaction. Again, Wold credits his success to the people who worked for and with him: his sales manager and the office manager who'd worked in a similar enterprise before joining Wolds.

"Through the years I've learned to give people responsibility and to encourage them to make good decisions. You can't do it alone and once you get a team that supports you — things can really happen."

Cliff believes that keeping active mentally helps keep him feeling and acting younger than his 88 years. He recommends this for all entrepreneurs, especially those over 50.

"Research carefully," he advises, "then give it all you've got. Making dreams come true does not come easy — but with united effort and many prayers, they can be realized."

IN CONCLUSION

You've read plenty of good advice from all of our business owners. They've shown you what they did to make their businesses successful. Now it is up to you to learn from their experiences and their advice. They've said over and over:

JUST GO DO IT!

The only person holding you back is you.

YOUR AGE IS AN ADVANTAGE!

A business of your own is a chance to use all the wisdom and experience you've gleaned through the years.

FREEDOM!

You'll have the freedom of no boss looking over your shoulder, no board telling you what to do, no time clock. And you'll also have the freedom to be creative, to serve your customers exactly as you think you should, to set your goals and make them happen.

DON'T BORROW!

You don't need the extra headaches and pressure.

SERVICE IS THE KEY TO SUCCESS!
Your customers will come back and bring others.

HAVE FUN WITH YOUR BUSINESS!
Do something you like; look forward to each day.

GOOD READING

The One Minute Manager by Kenneth Blanchard, Ph.D.
and Spencer Johnson, M.D., Berkley Books. If
business owners followed the suggestions in this
book, they probably wouldn't have to read any
others. And both they and their employees would
be happier.

LOOK FOR THESE TITLES IN OUR
MATURE READER SERIES:

OVER 50 AND STILL COOKING!
Recipes for Good Health and Long Life

THE NUTRITION GAME:
The Right Moves if You're Over 50

THE ENCYCLOPEDIA OF GRANDPARENTING
Hundreds of Ideas to Entertain Your
Grandchildren

DEALS AND DISCOUNTS
If You're 50 or Older

START YOUR OWN BUSINESS
AFTER 50 — OR 60 — OR 70!
These People Did. Here's How:

I DARE YOU!
How to Stay Young Forever

THE BEGINNER'S ANCESTOR RESEARCH KIT